IMAGES OF ENGLAND

CARLISLE REMEMBERED

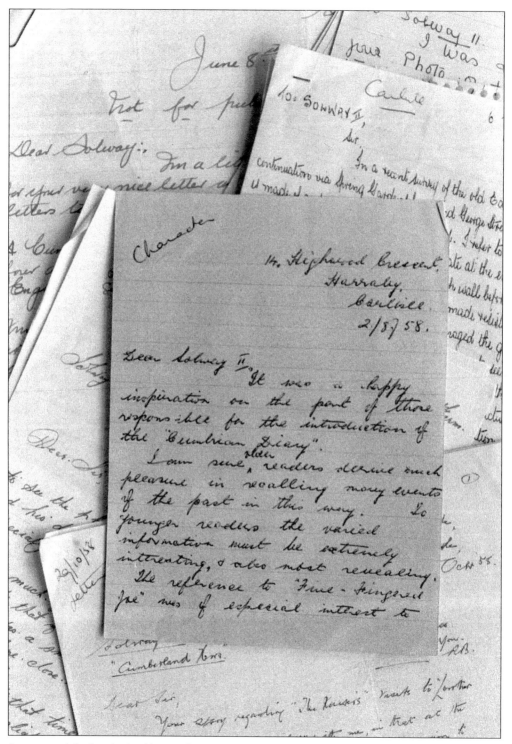

Just some of the hundreds of letters that Mary Burgess received as 'Solway II'. Her identity was never revealed in the column and she was often addressed as 'Dear Sir'.

IMAGES OF ENGLAND

CARLISLE REMEMBERED

DENIS PERRIAM

The
History
Press

First published 1999 by Tempus

Reprinted 2017 by
The History Press
The Mill, Brimscombe Port
Stroud, Gloucestershire, GL5 2QG
www.thehistorypress.co.uk

ISBN 978 0 7524 1678 6

Typesetting and origination by Tempus
Printed in Great Britain by TJ International Ltd, Padstow, Cornwall

Dedicated to the memory of
Mary Nelson Burgess 1910-1997
'Solway II'

Cover picture: A circus procession along Castle Street in the 1890s.

CONTENTS

Frederick John Parker ('Dapper-Dick'), 1880-1973. He regularly wrote to Mary Burgess in his retirement at Keswick. He was brought up in Carlisle and had many childhood memories of the city. This is him aged twenty-four, in 1904. He took charge of J.G. Parker's ironmongers, in Botchergate, at the age of sixteen, when his father died suddenly.

INTRODUCTION

Mary Burgess wrote a weekly local history column in the *Cumberland News* under the pseudonym 'Solway II', between 1955 and 1978. During this time she received hundreds of letters every year on all aspects of Cumbrian history. Many letters came from far away places, written by people who had left the area but had rich memories of their birthplace. These letters are a unique resource for the local historian and are destined for the Cumbria Record Office. This book is intended to make the memories more widely known.

It would be impossible to include every letter in full, so extracts from those only relating to the Carlisle area have been included, with the minimum of editorial input.

Many of the correspondents were born in the 1870s and 1880s. They could remember the city when Queen Victoria was on the throne. One man had been to London to celebrate the Queen's Diamond Jubilee in 1897; another could remember marching through cheering crowds in the city on his way to fight in the Boer War. A Carlisle choir was in

Carlisle Covered Market was always busy on Saturdays, particularly at this time – the 1890s.

Paris when the *Titanic* sank and they were asked to sing the hymn sung by those who went down with the ship; one youth joined the Army and was in the trenches of the First World War when he was still only fifteen.

There are lighter moments: a woman remembered an escaped monkey causing havoc in her home at Upperby; the man who survived putting his head in a lion's mouth, and the woman who never thought that the day would come when women could buy ready-made trousers.

Memories were often triggered by photographs which Mary Burgess reproduced in her column. Most of these pictures were treasured possessions and were faithfully returned after use, but it has been possible to locate some of them to illustrate the book. Other illustrations have been chosen from a number of collections, most reproduced for the first time.

Annual street processions featured horse-drawn floats, the horses adorned with brightly polished brasses. Here the Little White Ribboners set off from the County Garage on one of James Robinson's carts in the 1920s.

ACKNOWLEDGEMENTS

Dr Patt Honeyman passed the letters to me at the suggestion of Mary Burgess in 1996. I am grateful to them both for giving me this opportunity to study the letters in the comfort of my own home. I also thank Patt Honeyman for making pictures from his own collection available for reproduction.

Mary Burgess included extracts from the letters in her column in the *Cumberland News* and I am grateful to Robin Burgess, Chief Executive of the Cumbrian Newspaper Group (and nephew of Miss Burgess) for allowing the letters to be used for publication. I am also grateful for permission to use *Cumberland News* photographs stored in Cumbria Record Office. I am grateful to the staff of the Record Office for making available both photographs and material in the Mary Burgess collection. I thank Anne Cartmell for permission to use this collection.

Other photographs are from my own collection and from Ashley Kendall, John Huggon, Tullie House Museum & Art Gallery, Carlisle Library, Kevin Rafferty, John Parker, Mrs J. Saul, John Routledge, John L. Underwood, and Anthony Sewell.

Thanks also to the many correspondents who wrote in, most of them are now dead but their memories bring history alive! This book is also a tribute to them.

Denis Perriam, 1999

CHAPTER 1

Childhood

Motor cars were rarely seen in Carlisle in the Edwardian era and a parked car like this one in Eden Street could quickly draw a crowd of admiring children. This Humber was registered in December 1910 by Mrs Ada Young of St Aidan's Road.

The Woman With A Nose

I have had seventy years of memory, not bad for a kid that was wrapped up in a bundle at the age of two weeks (so I was told) as of no further use… not expected [to live]. I was born in 1886, coming to live in Collingwood Street, Denton Holme, from Milbourn Street at the age of three in 1889. Many characters I knew…in Milbourn Street for instance there was an old woman known as the 'woman with a nose'. As a kid of two or three years old all of us were scared stiff and used to run in the house and lock the doors. She used to pinch the cat and dogs dinners.

George (Danny) Doyle, 1958

Johnnie Bulldog's Lonning

I was born in 1885 and when a very little girl we went to live at the house at the Warwick Road end of the Lonning [which led to the river]. My father was Johnnie Wallace and had a great big yellow mastiff (as big as a horse) and very savage. It was kept on a chain. I remember children being told, 'if you go down there Johnnie's bulldog will get you'.

Mrs Herbert, 1956

Johnnie Mac Elroy's Dog

About the 1820s a man the name of John Richardson came from Northumberland to live in the cottage and built sheds for workshops to make Richardson's winnowing machines for cleaning grain. My father was brought up at Botcherby and was bound apprentice with Mr Richardson but when the business grew they moved into the city. Then a man the name of Johnnie MacElroy lived there and it was he that had the bulldog and put up the sign on the end of the shed 'Beware of the Dog'. After he died the Wallaces came to live there. I knew the Wallaces and also their big yellow dog. It was the city people that christened the lonning 'Johnnie Bulldog's Lonning'. The real name was Botcherby Holm Lonning and the lonning ended at a gate into Ambrose Holm, which was a very big field.

Robert Johnson, February 1956

Beware of the Dog

There never was a dog, at least from 1890, just a painted tin plate 'Beware of the Dog', which we boys felt sure was to prevent us from raiding the orchard, but did it? I ask you.

Fred Parker, 1956

Hangings

How pleased I was to see…a picture of the Victoria Hotel in English Street…Mr and Mrs C.J. Armstrong …was my father and mother and I was born there on 28 December 1880. Mr and Mrs Campbell were tenants previous to my father and mother taking it over and my mother was a niece of theirs…I can remember as just a little boy [in 1886] with my mother

The Victoria Hotel, seen on the right in this 1880s view, was demolished in 1904 for rebuilding. Across the street on the left is the County Gaol wall and the flagpole for the black flag.

watching through a window of the hotel when the black flag was hoisted in Carlisle Gaol after the execution of Rudge, Martin and Baker, the Netherby burglars. In fact Baker's father stayed at the hotel during the assize trial. I can also remember the days when the Carlisle troop of the Westmorland & Cumberland Yeomanry used to assemble in front of the hotel before proceeding by road to Lowther Park to do their annual summer training. Really it is nice to recall the good old Victorian days.

James Beaty, September 1965

Reading

One very personal event for me was the opening of the public library [at Tullie House in 1893]. I was only eleven and the impact was important for I acquired a deep love of reading which I've enjoyed my long life.

James Beaty, September 1965

Skating On The Eden

I was thrilled to see the picture, skating on the River Eden in the year 1895, as I remember it well…My da took me there to see the people skating, we stood

11

The severe winter of 1895 resulted in the River Eden being frozen for a number of weeks. Skaters were to be seen on the ice each day, here on 21 February.

a while watching and then da and me went on and we had a jolly good time. I was seven years of age then, but I never forgot as it was a lovely sight to see. I could stand the cold better then, as da and me have walked for miles in the cold on frosty days.

Mrs M. Cubby, December 1962

Train-spotting

Barwise Nook was a train-spotter's paradise, there is no doubt. I can remember the LNER steam cars *Nettle* and *Flower of Yarrow* which ran to Port Carlisle and later to Langholm. The three huge Pacific locomotives which were shedded at the canal, *Colorado*, *Flamingo* and *Captain Cuttle*. These were the giants of their day. It was a

sight worth seeing, to see one of these large green locomotives makings its way slowly around the curve, tender first, the sun glinting on the boiler and rippling on the spokes of the driving wheels, heading for the station to pick up a train. Those majestic machines were kept clean in those days [early 1930s].

D. Laing, March 1976

Engines and Cars

I could never have believed that a pastime in which I engaged well upwards of fifty years ago would have survived all through the years. As boys we (living in Denton Holme) would cross to the Currock side of the Caldew, climb and straddle the high-board fence by the railway and we would sit with note book and pencil and record the engine numbers. But one thing we never attempted was to get down on the railway side of the fence and get near the tracks. We were very conscious that it would be trespassing. In those same days, cars being a novelty and being not too numerous we got as much pleasure from recording their licence numbers, when we went along the streets, as we did from taking engine numbers.

Stan Goldsworthy, September 1960

Floods

I was born in Barwise Nook in 1921, one of an eventual family of six, so all the early days of my childhood were spent there…One of my earliest recollections, it must have been in the region of 1925, was when the adjacent Caldew, after heavy rains, overflowed its banks and flooded the whole area, up into Caldewgate, to a depth of some feet in places. On this occasion two men in a rowing boat came down Willow Holme, *en route* for the sewerage, or filter beds, to rescue two men who were marooned on the roof there, who had been working on the night shift. On this occasion however, the council made a free issue of coal to the downstairs tenants to help with the drying up. The 'Nook' suffered another flood [in 1931], but we were luckier this time because we lived upstairs. I remember my father wading up Willow Holme in water up to his waist, another man, shorter then

One of the Pacific locomotives, *Sir Visto*, of the same class as referred to by Mr Laing. It is pictured at the Canal Shed with a retired engine driver, showing the scale of the loco.

Flooded Church Street, Caldewgate, in January 1925 – the event remembered by Mr Laing.

he, hanging on to his jacket. A man couldn't afford to stay away from work. But flooding didn't happen very often.

D. Laing, March 1976

The City Police

One day I saw a policeman in English Street with a goose under his arm. I thought it was a strange thing.

Miss M.A. Armstrong, October 1956

The Fat Policeman

The constable well known to us all [as children] was PC Blake who I understand topped the twenty stone mark. His family shop was a butcher's business situated at the corner of Bridge Lane, Caldewgate…This locality contained some of the toughest

characters…When full of drink some of the dealer fraternity, locally known as 'Potter Diddles', used to tease or goad Blake by remarks, or getting up close and saying 'come and get me copper', to which Blake eyeing them tersely would reply 'Mind ah canna run- but ah can hod [hold]'. [Later] some of my friends were in the force, PC Tom Senior, Sergeants Bill Oliver and Tom Smith.

Harold Slight, 1962

The Lamp Lighter

Being the octogenarian that I am, I remember the pre-pilot [light] days when the entire actual lighting of [street] lamps had to be done by a lamp lighter. The long pole had a slotted end by which to turn on the 'bare' gas and the same pole-end carried a lighted taper, so that immediately the gas was turned on it was ignited by the flame from the taper. Very seldom did the light of the taper become extinguished *en route* from one light-standard to another.

Stan Goldsworth, July 1974

Top Hats

My grandfather, Thomas Wilson, had a bonny tenor voice, although after he left the Cathedral Choir [in 1909], he very rarely sang. He was an imposing figure in my boyhood days – not very tall, a beard and always on a Sunday clothed in a frock coat and top hat. How long would a top hat last these days?

Tom Wilson, November 1960

Chinamen and Red Indians

My memory goes back to the 1880s. Lowther Street at that time was not a thoroughfare. The street then terminated a few yards beyond Spring Gardens in a short steep incline to the level of the house still standing on the right and then occupied by Alderman Denard. Across the roadway, as far as memory serves, were iron railings and gate, beyond which a cobbled pathway, with a row of houses and gardens on the left, led to Swifts Row. Beyond Swifts Row lay the Sands eight or ten feet below present level, a quagmire in winter and on it the Matchbox, a large wooden structure, originally a music hall but by then (1886) used by the Salvation Army and in which I had the thrill of seeing pig-tailed Chinamen

and Red Indians in war regalia during an international congress of Salvation Army adherents.

J.J. Proudfoot, November 1960

The Stick Men

Other friends of ours were the stickmen who used to deliver firewood to us at our home in Aglionby Street, where we had wonderful cellars, including one given over entirely to [wood] blocks and our winter stock of peat.

Anne Johnson, June 1969

William Oliver came from Matlock, Derbyshire, to join the city police on 2 October 1897. He retired with the rank of sergeant in 1923.

Peat

Well I remember the old woman who came into Botchergate and sold blocks of peat like a brick at eight or nine a penny. She had come all the way from Scaleby with a pony nearly as old as herself and I have bought them there before going to school

William Johnston, May 1957

Pocket Money

Coals. I have wheeled from Binnings in Denton Street many a ton at 7d a hundred weight. If you asked for 'small', 5d a hundred weight and when

Old Cottage at Houghton, Carlisle.   Thos Bushby

The pond at Houghton in 1907, much as Mr Reed remembered it.

you took the 'barrer' [barrow] back, you had left a deposit of 1d, it was yours for 'fetching' the coals. That, by the way, was our only source of income [as children].

George (Danny) Doyle, 1958

Funny Times

Yesterday I celebrated my eighty-ninth birthday and can remember quite well the paper entitled *Funny Times*. There was one in front of that called The *Border Standard* which the young ones liked much better. *Funny Times* was not quite as nice so it soon dropped out.

Elizabeth Story, April 1960

Houghton

I was born at Houghton in 1915, in the house known as Larch House which stood overlooking the pond (now filled in), the green and village hall. Geese always roamed the green in those days. A Mr Hetherington farmed next to us on the south side and opposite stood the old village pump. On the north side of our house, nearest the village store was a farm owned by Mr Errington. Mr Robinson was in charge of the village store. He and my father, Edward Secker Reed, were in charge of the Sunday school in the little Methodist chapel, now a shop. The farm facing down the green and adjoining the store was occupied by a Mr Sutton. Opposite the store was a little cottage where Ally Errington, the blacksmith

Steam threshing, thought to be at Low Longthwaite Farm near Wigton in 1906. The traction engine is hard at work operating the thresher on the right.

lived. Above [beyond] the post office another farm occupied by a Mr Byers. The postmistress was Miss Errington who took over from her mother Ann Errington. Houghton as I knew it has faded into the past. The old smithy has disappeared, but the school I first attended remains, rather dilapidated. Another character I remember was Old Isaac the roadman, whom I have seen crawling along on his hands and knees pulling out weeds on the edge of the road through the village.

Lawrence Secker Reed, August 1969

Warts

When quite a young girl I had a big ugly wart on my wrist and on asking the old midwife about it, was told to put a length of black cotton in a hiding place outside, no one but myself to know, and visit the place each evening after sunset and tie a knot in the cotton and replace in the hiding place. Well I did so for a few evenings and one morning my mother said, 'And what about your wart?' I looked at my wrist and it was gone completely.

Mrs Mildred Edwards, January 1959

Harvest Time

Eden Joy was the old steam engine that used to come round Cargo with the corn thresher when I was a boy. I started school when I was three years old, way back in 1913 and as far as I can remember it did not look to be a new engine then. So if it is still around then it must be a good ripe old age. When I first remembered it, a man called Jimmy Burrows used to drive it and a chap called Geordy Storr was his assistant. They came every so often and most of us school kids went to see

17

The City Arms, decorated for the coronation of Edward VII in 1902. This pub was remembered by its nickname, the Gaol Tap. The gaol gateway can be seen on the left and the Prince of Wales feathers at roof level, the trade mark of Worthingtons.

it and play around it whenever it came to Cargo. Both of them knew us all by our names. The thresher used to stay in the village for quite a while…mostly in autumn and winter months. It went round nearly all the farms. It was quite a busy time for everyone on the farm, both male and female. It made good friendships and sharing spirit amongst the farmers. They all turned in to help out at whichever farm the thresher was at. They could not have managed otherwise. It might sound disgusting but we went to catch and kill the mice and rats. There were always dozens of them all sizes, some still in their nests, mostly at the bottom of the stack.

Willie McCormick, November 1975

Threshing

Jim Burrows and my father, Georgie Storr, were partners in the threshing business in the very early years. My father eventually had four sets of steam-tackle on the road which were sold at Durdar when he retired about 1919.

T. Storr, November 1975

Gaol Tap

All my young life it was known as the Gaol Tap, with the late John Minns as the licensee…a glorious looking building it was too, when it had the Prince of Wales feathers all gilded and decorated up for special occasions; these seemed to be John Minns' great joy. By the way, I wonder what became of the group of statutory in the tiara [pediment] – just smashed up I suppose?

Mildred Edwards, April 1970

which he proceeded to do with great fervour. He had his Bible in his hand and being carried away by his prayerful enthusiasm, he brought the sacred volume down in a series of whacks upon my head.

Tom Lightfoot, March 1957

Ranters

Of ranters, I well remember such local stalwarts as Ward Parker, Johnny Barnes, Fred Moor and others, marching from the Primitive Methodist chapel, Upperby, to the city boundary singing with great gusto *The Lion of Judah shall break every chain*, to the wonderment of we small boys. I once attended a cottage meeting where some of these gentlemen were present. One of them, who was seated behind me, was called upon to offer prayer

Grandfather

At 68 Lowther Street lived my grandfather, Joseph Denard and his family. As well as being in business at 74-76 Lowther Street as a painter and decorator, he was a councillor, alderman and, I believe, a member, if not chairman of the Watch Committee. I have heard my father, Charles Denard, speak of these things. My grandfather was bedfast for a number of years before his death and I remember quite vividly as a child being thrilled by the long

Joseph Denard's premises on Lowther Street. One of his specialities was painting and decorating churches.

The Plaza Ballroom, as remembered by Miss Denard, where 'flappers' learned to dance. This was situated in the former Albert Hall on Chapel Street.

cheval mirror which was so placed in his bedroom that he could see the comings and goings; military parades, band and fancy dress processions etc., as they traversed Victoria Place. Later the house was occupied by Madame Stockdale, teacher of dancing, who ran the old Plaza Ballroom in Chapel Street. This is doubtless remembered by many staid and respectable fathers and mothers and indeed, grandfathers and grandmothers of today, who were the young men about town and the flappers of those days.

Miss J.O. Denard, April 1958

Windy Days

One of my favourite pastimes was to stand at the corner of Warwick Road and the Crescent on a windy day and see how many umbrellas were blown inside out and watch the expression on some of the faces. Some would tuck it under their arm and some would throw them away. This is what you call a youthful pastime!

C. Armstrong

Friends

My name was Kennedy and my special friend was Ruth Little. We were hardly ever separated. My mother brought most of the Littles into the world.

Ella Middleton, March 1959

A Lovely Lady

Many a time I saw Miss Thwaites sketching all over town and used to stand and watch her. She used to talk to me. When I told her I was in St Paul's choir she gave me 2d. She was a lovely lady. I can picture her now, in her white straw hat (I think they called them 'Lyhorns' those days), white blouse and navy skirt.

J. Ferguson, November 1957

A Love of Art

I am not an artist, but Miss Slee and the late James Atherton taught me at the Higher Grade [school] and at least instilled a love of art. I always thought Miss Slee had a magical gift of transforming the humdrum into a thing of beauty. Her neat clean lines and wonderfully accurate perspective was her special gift.

Mrs Margaret M. Scott, December 1958

High School

I was eight years old and the youngest pupil when the Girls High School opened at 19 Castle Street in 1884 (January). I remained at the school for seven years. The teachers were excellent and the education I received has been most valuable in the work I have done since I left. I very much enjoyed the Jubilee celebrations and I shall look forward to celebrating the seventy-five years.

Miss E. Barnes, May 1959

Oldest Pupil

I believe I am the oldest surviving pupil who attended Carlisle High School when it first opened. I recall the large school gardens where the children rushed out helter-skelter to play ball games and to skip. At the very beginning I was a resident pupil, but later I used to travel back and forth daily by pony and trap. The pony was called 'Tiny' – a spirited little animal that was brought from over the Border. There was no school uniform as such, but the little ones mostly wore pinafores and the headmistress, Miss Bain, maintained her dignity with a primly befrilled bonnet and ankle-length black dress. At this time, aged about nine, I wore my dark hair short and 'shingled', but many of the other girls had long hair, some with 'corkscrew' curls, not like some of today's hair fashions.

Mrs Ethel Inglis

Ragged School

I think it was a great pity that the old Ragged School, a worthy memorial to the Head family, should have been so ruthlessly destroyed. In comparison to the Tithe Barn which really is of no historical value, as it was simply a storage for grain demanded by the church. This school was a pioneer in creating education for the poor and should have been preserved.

Mrs Margaret M. Scott, February 1964

Empire Day

As a family we attended Ashley Street School. Starting at five years old the classes were mixed, until about the age of nine, when boys went 'up' to the Boys' and girls went to the Girls' School. It was the same school, only divided by iron railings in the schoolyard and of course different classrooms. A big day at school those days [late 1920s], was Empire Day, when the whole school, in their respective classes, all stood in the schoolyard for about an hour and sang patriotic songs such as *Hurrah for the dear old Union Jack, Wales, Wales, Land of My Fathers* and *Land of Hope and Glory*. Immediately after the session was finished we were all sent home for the day wearing our Union Jacks. We had to take our own flag of course. A small one cost a penny and were always available in toy shops, as were whips and tops, pea shooters, etc. There always seemed to be certain times of the year when the latter were on sale.

D. Laing, May 1976

The Paris Choir

In the photograph of the Goodwin Boys' School Choir visit to the Paris Musical Festival in 1912, I am the boy in the light-coloured suit behind the right shoulder of Mr W.H. Reid, who was in fact my father. Detailed recollections of this tremendous adventure are, of course, somewhat hazy after fifty years, but I have often, in retrospect, marvelled at the efficiency of its organization. Everything was effectively laid on beforehand and I can

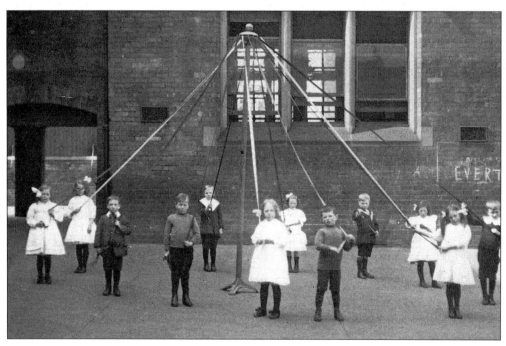

Ashley Street School with the children around the maypole. From chalk graffiti on the wall, in this pre-First World War view, it is apparent that someone supported Everton.

The Bishop Goodwin Boys Choir at school after their success in Paris in 1912.

recall no flaps, nor did anyone get lost. The choir was divided into groups of six boys, each having a leader whose job it was to keep them together and as part of the main party. At every railway station or other rallying point, the group leader simply stood still and bawled his group number at the top of his voice until all his charges had flocked round him like chickens round a broody hen. Some of the teachers came with us, although the only one I can clearly recall was Mr J. Scales, who taught Standard 5 and who was reputed among us boys, to be a fluent French linguist. It is my recollection however, that he did not seem altogether happy in the role of interpreter!

We did a little sight-seeing in London on the outward journey, including a visit to the House of Commons: then had a slap-up meal in a private room in some hotel or restaurant and were greatly intrigued at being served by waiters in 'tails'. We were also supplied with packed meals to eat on the boat, but as the Channel was a bit choppy nobody felt much like eating and most of the packed meals went overboard, either before or after ingestion…my new raincoat was never quite the same again!

Once in Paris we were accommodated in a boarding school at Vincennes, in the suburbs. Most of the French schoolboys were on holiday, but a few were still living at the school during the holidays. We were greatly amused at their closely shorn hair and somewhat contemptuous of their puny stature and general lack of pep. Every endeavour to inveigle them into our games was received with apparent apprehension and we thought them a pretty poor lot. What they thought of us, of course, we never knew.

We slept at nights in one of the school dormitories – a huge bare room with two long rows of beds – which was a new experience for us. I recall that on the first night we had some difficulty in settling down and there were some tears from a few who were a bit homesick, overtired or perhaps just overwhelmed by the excitement of events. Our teachers – as well as my mother who had come with us – staying in the dormitory administering comfort or reprimand as the case might warrant until we all finally slept.

One of the French schoolmasters – an excitable little character with a brand of English entirely peculiar to himself – acted as our guide on our various sightseeing excursions…[nicknamed] 'Gas Bill'. The competition itself was held in a huge hall or theatre and my only recollection of it is vague and confusing. We were not impressed, I recall, by the singing of the French childrens' choirs, whose voices sounded thin, nasal and harsh, but in spite of this, we only managed to pull off second prize in the set pieces. The sight-singing test was, however a piece of cake to those of us who had sight-reading drummed into us by 'WH' from the moment we first entered the school.

The trophies we won came into my possession on the death of my father and I have them still. Awarded for the second prize in the test pieces was a circlet of gilt laurel leaves and for the sight-reading a silver plaque which bears the inscription, 'Bishop Road, Carlisle'. This careless error by the Paris Festival authorities annoyed my father immensely and further aggravated the typically insular

prejudice he had always held against all things 'foreign'.

A.W. Reid, June 1962

The Titanic

I've been in Canada since 1923… but was a member of the Goodwin Boys' Paris Choir. I well remember our trip to Paris. At that age who could forget it! It was wonderful and everyone was so kind. Mr W. Reid, the choirmaster and head of the school was an inspiration to all. 'Bogie' as we called him, was beloved by all his boys. At Paris we were housed in a school on the outskirts of the city. The time being shortly after the sinking of the *Titanic*. This particular evening, we had just retired, when Mr Reid entered the dormitory and said the residents and staff of the school would like us to sing the hymn that had been sung when the *Titanic* was sinking. This we did. All of us in our sleeping attire, sitting up in bed, singing *Nearer My God To Thee*, something I will never forget.

William J. Harrison, February 1963

Choir School

In my boyhood as a chorister in Carlisle Cathedral, I sang under Dr Wadely from 1925 to 1932…Dr Wadely had in fact originated from Kidderminster. What a great man he was and despite the strict regime, how we boys loved him. The interest he took in us all, mostly from humble homes and the dedication and happiness we

Choir boys grouped behind a colour party from the Border Regiment in 1914, outside the main entrance to the cathedral. No evidence here of muddy football boots.

gave him and got in return. The time when I broke my wrists falling from a chestnut tree in Rickerby Park and had to spend several weeks in the Infirmary being visited and spoon-fed by FW. Then six of the best for sticking chewing gum on Sammy Barrett's hair. Rushing up from playing football on the Bitts on a Saturday afternoon, still in muddy football boots, just in time for Mr Sharp to spit on his hand and slick my hair back and push a cassock and surplice over my head for me to carry the Cross in front of Dean Stuart up the aisle on the last bell of four for another evensong! Service over, FW glancing down at my boots and saying 'At least you might kick the mud off William before coming into God's Holy Place'.

William Underwood, October 1976

Late for School

To get to Ashley Street School from Barwise Nook, I could use the footpath behind Carr's Biscuit Works. If more than one of you went to school at the same time, the journey was usually spent in a game of 'handicaps' or 'cuppies'. The leader of the party would climb a gate or a tree and jump and the rest had to follow suit. We were often late for school! Carr's hooter would blow at twenty-five past one and then we had to run to school, before they blew their second one at half-past. For after that you were late.

D. Laing, May 1976

Never Absent

25

The May Queen and her attendants on Priory Road in the late twenties.

In 1906 I was awarded a medal for perfect attendance 'never absent, never late'. At that time I was a pupil at Stanwix School, Mulcaster Crescent and was twelve years of age. I still have this medal.

Ethel Thurlow (née Brown), June 1959

May Queens

An event which is worthy of note, I think, was the electing of the 'May Queen', which seemed to be carried out in each street in those days. The particular occasion which I mention was the year [about 1930] my younger sister, then aged about five years, was elected. There was great preparations, ribbons, old lace curtain for the queen's train and fancy dress for her attendants. The great day arriving, they all paraded around the different yards and ended up in the street [Barwise Nook] for the banquet.

Neighbours had all brought out their kitchen tables and chairs. The tables were placed end to end, down the centre of the street, covered with white cloths or white sheets and everyone sat down to tea and cakes. These had been paid for by money raised by collections around the houses. The cakes had been purchased at Willie Allan's a well-known baker's in Caldewgate. During the beano [there was] music on the melodeon and games afterwards. There was always something going on in 'The Nook'.

D. Laing, May 1976

CHAPTER 2

Hard times

Jimmy Dyer was a musician who composed his own songs and sold them in sheet form around the streets. Here he is in the Market Place with a young audience.

Strikes

In the 1900s there occurred to my memory...three strikes. I believe the one at Carr's Biscuit Works was caused by the action of a forewoman who found fault with a young operative. There was a report that after striking the girl, she threatened her with suspension. Out streamed the workers to a mass meeting held outside the gates. Then came the decision to stay out until the matter was settled by a workers' delegation and the directors. After some days the directors quashed the case, but in the interim there were ugly evening scenes at the home of the forewoman in Water Street. Extra police were called in to disperse the large crowd. It was fortunate that there weren't any stones in this vicinity.

The next was, believe it or not, the paper sellers of the *East Cumberland News*, who were led by the eldest, a chap called 'Paddy' who made an impassioned speech at the Cross. He made the request for a further halfpenny on each dozen papers sold. They succeeded in their quest.

Finally it was the turn of Hudson Scott's employees, who came out when their piece rates were drastically cut. This was settled within an hour or two. It took grit and spirit in those days, for there were no funds of any description. Even living was precarious.

Harold Slight, 1964

No Dinner

Soup kitchens were opened when the big coal strike was on and the trains stopped running. I think this was while Mr Creighton was mayor [1926]. We lived at Currock at that time and at the school my daughter went to, the children were asked to put their hands up if they had had no dinner and Mary put her hand up. The teacher said 'Ho! Mary, so you've had no dinner', and she replied ' No, my mother was washing so we just had bacon and eggs'. She thought that if we had no potatoes it was not a dinner!

Signed 'an old member of the Charlotte Street church', February 1958

Hunger

I've heard of a family so desperate that they took a pram to a field and killed a sheep. They covered it over in the pram like a child and came back through the streets, past the police who never spotted them. Some of this would be cooked and eaten when they got home.

Jas Maxwell, 1957

Toys For Poor Children

The line of children outside Charlotte Street Congregational church were there to receive toys. I recognize the little fellow walking across the street grasping the toy sword as myself. I don't know who sponsored the gifts, but one had to have a ticket to receive a toy...receiving the sword is still very vivid in my mind

Thomas Bulman, February 1958

Children wait outside of Charlotte Street Congregational church in 1911 for Christmas gifts. Some of those not in the queue here have already received their toys.

Christmas Gifts

I have discovered that the photograph of the children outside Charlotte Street was for the distributing of toys to poor children by the mayor, 23 December 1911.

Revd Harry Smith, February 1958

Christmas For The Poor

The Christmas dinners for the poor were largely organized by the late John Bell – who also provided most of the cost, in as much as he provided a prize bullock each year. This used to be displayed at Mark's butcher's shop, Portland Place, for some days. The dinners comprised of a potato pot – these were made by a band of volunteers and cooked in a number of public bake houses with the old brick ovens. Tickets were distributed and each household collected their own dinner – the bake tins were returned when each received ½lb tea in exchange. There was also another annual event at Christmas – a tea for 400-500 children in the Drill Hall, the tickets for which were given out by School Attendance Officers and the police force. Each child on leaving received an apple, a bag of sweets and a new penny. No one knew who were the donors of this 'feast' and it would be wrong for me to break the trust today.

Fred Parker, January 1969

29

Cottage Children's Home

I would like to confirm that a country cottage home for children of Carlisle did materialize, as I was probably one of the first children to be in residence in March 1912. It was situated at Cumdivock and the lady in charge was called Mrs Porthouse. Also the cook-housemaid was called Sarah. We were taken for walks, one being to a farm, farmed by people called Guardhouse. Also to some people called Bragg and they kept bees. Mr Bragg was a woodcutter and they had two children, Harry and Linda. As it was sixty-one years ago I am not sure of the organizers names apart from a Miss Martindale and the offices were in Chapel Street. While I was at the home a Mrs Stead from Dalston Hall presented a huge dolls house for the children to play with. I hope someone else will remember the happy days spent there,

Miss M. Murphy, September 1973

The Clog Fund

Our city police force…in the era 1890 to 1930…were above all very human to the poor of that time. The policemen made personal weekly contributions every winter to a Clog Fund. Such was the hardship of the youth of the day, they could be seen wearing galoshes or slippers in the coldest weather. They ran the Police Ball in the spacious County Hall every winter in aid of the Clog Fund.

Harold Slight, 1962

Gas and Electricity

It was very difficult for many of the mothers who had neither gas nor electricity in their house – a fire had to be lighted in quite the wee small hours in order to be in a fit state to be cooked upon.

Mrs Marjorie Slade, June 1967

Tramps Breakfasts

These free meals, popularly known as 'The Tramps Breakfast' were held on Sunday mornings in a hall in Peter Street and were largely attended. It was undertaken by a number of Christian friends in the city interested in the welfare of destitute wayfarers and the like and was supported by voluntary contributions. The company was of a cosmopolitan character and I can recall on more than one occasion having had pointed out to me one-time professional men who, unfortunately, had fallen on evil days.

After the meal, which consisted of mugs of hot tea and a plentiful supply of wholesome food, there was a short gospel service and some hymn singing. With improved living conditions and the comparative absence of the familiar tramp of the road, the Carlisle Sunday Morning Free Breakfast association came to a close following the First World War.

David J. Beattie, November 1955

The Revd G. Bramwell Evens, seen here in 1925, was a Wesleyan minister, but he enjoyed living like a tramp in a gypsy caravan. He is better known to many as 'Romany', the naturalist, who thrilled children with programs for the BBC.

Bandmaster Hugh Kerr, in his smart uniform, stands with the Harraby Hill House Band in Hartington Street, outside Wood View. The album from which this came is dated March 1911 to June 1913. Moffitt Brothers sold 'sarks' (shirts) in their outfitter's shops. This 'Sark Parade', as William Moffitt called it, was to advertise the opening of a new shop on English Street, but for some reason it was banned by the city council.

Orphan Bands

As one who played in the Harraby Hill House Band…it brings back memories of happy times. Mr Kerr, the bandmaster, was very smart in his uniform; also was very patient in learning us boys. The band was in great demand at local flower shows and village fêtes. We also played at Brunton Park in the football season for about five seasons. We often marched around Carlisle playing for collections for many good causes. For many summers we played in the bandstand in the park. In regard to the Chadwick Band we often felt some rivalry between us. We had a song which went like this:

'The Chadwick is not so good
The Harraby get lots of food
And if they come to Bell's Field
We shall show them football too'.

Tom Murray, 1969

Rivals

Several of the members of the Harraby Hill House Band were in my class at St John's School, which I attended until 1909, when I moved to Yorkshire. Quite a number of the bandsmen joined the regular army and played in regimental bands.

There was a lot of rivalry between the 'House' and Chadwick Memorial School Bands and they played at the football matches on alternate seasons. You will realise that there was much gloom among the House boys when it was Chadwick's turn. Incidentally the House band was a brass band and Chadwick's a military band with the usual woodwind instruments etc.

Jimmy Bell, July 1969

Bandmasters

My father, Hugh James Kerr, was a master painter and decorator. His spare time he gave to Harraby Hill boys as their bandmaster. When they moved to Shap [in 1916], he went every Saturday for practice or to take the boys to play at different places. My father unfortunately died at the age of forty-four years in 1923. My brother Charles, took over the band temporarily until John Ruddick was appointed. This gentleman was with the Boys Band until it was disbanded [in the 1930s].

Norah Kerr, August 1969

Working For Breakfast

A farmer on the Wigton Road near Carlisle had a good scheme. He sometimes had as many as six tramps some nights. He locked them in the barn where they slept. He let them out in the morning and they had to do some work, cleaning byres etc. for their breakfast and off they went.

Jas Maxwell, 1957

Cheap Bacon Man

I wonder how many folks remember John Linton, 'the Cheap Bacon Man'. He used to get on the top step [of the Market Cross] and lay down the law to some tune. He used to get pelted with all sorts of rubbish, but he still talked on.

J. Ferguson, November 1957

Gypsies

A band of Serbian gypsies sometimes stayed in one of the lonnings, swarthy complexions and the women wore big brass earrings. They were organ grinders, organs on wheels and shafts for a pony.

Jas Maxwell, 1957

Five-fingered Joe

Five-fingered Joe was long before my time but my mother knew him by repute and she used to tell me about him. Apparently he hailed from Dalston district and on his excursions into town would do any shopping for anyone and take his purchases back with him in an old-fashioned wicker basket.

Miss E. Armstrong, August 1958

Five-fingered Joe, seen here late in life, posed in the studio of J. Monk on Charlotte Street. He had a basket, which he used when he went shopping in Carlisle for Dalston folk.

Chadwick Memorial School, now Austin Friars, saw a number of uses after opening in 1892. For the first eleven years it was a convent school run by The Order of the Sacred Heart and these are some of the pupils.

Calling Names

Five-fingered Joe and Caul Yale were both drovers, a common occupation, since cattle in those days were driven through the streets. Five-fingered Joe, so called because he actually had five fingers and a thumb on each hand, was a little chap. He wore a rough serge suit with a deep jacket and bulging pockets. He always carried an extra long stick with which to urge on his charges. Boys would shout after him 'Five-fingered Joe', then bolt for he was an angry man when roused. Caul Yale was a simpler, inoffensive character. He got his nickname because of his practice of asking for a glass of 'caul yale' (cold ale) when treated to a drink. I don't remember him retaliating when the teasing habits of boys made him their victim.

James Beaty, July 1958

Nanny Knockabout

I knew Nanny Knockabout as a child in the early years of this century. We were living at Carleton then and she came begging. I don't remember her selling anything. She wore lots of petticoats, red under and black over, often with a black braid stitched on them. She carried a billy can and drank from the lid. She used to pat my friend Gladys and I on the head and say 'Yer two fine bairns'. My father used to smile and say 'She's the nearest thing to a walking tent I've ever seen'. My mother once asked her if she came from these parts, but all she said was 'I'm yen of the Armstrongs'. She was really on the roads and slept in barns.

An OAP, February 1960

A Walking Haystack

I remember that she never tried to sell anything. I can also vividly remember that she resembled a walking haystack… her garb was usually two or three overcoats worn over numerous skirts and petticoats, a pair of men's shoes, an old black straw hat trimmed around with cock tail feathers. She carried a sack over her shoulder and a large umbrella, usually put up, not to protect her head but carried under her arm, keeping her rear either dry or shaded from the sun.

Many a wet afternoon she spent sitting in our washhouse and many a lecture she gave my mother on the bringing up of children. She once said she had a farmer brother whom she used to call on at odd times but apparently got very little encouragement from her sister-in-law whom she described as a 'feckless body'. 'They want nowt wi me, thou knows' she used to say.

At that time she was camping out in a hut built of sackings, bits of wood and broken sheets of old corrugated iron. She got little peace from the schoolchildren who teased and plagued her unmercifully…but she was always kind to me. I remember one morning my schoolfellows all ran away and left me and Nannie emerged from her lair in the middle of some high whins on a piece of waste ground near Newby Cross. 'Has the tatty rubbish left thu' she said. 'Well, ah must see thu safely to school'. And despite my struggles, she grasped my hand and escorted me right through the school yard up to the school door [at Cummersdale], amid the jeers and laughter of the children. 'Theer now', she said 'A'll be waiting for tha when thu comes out the night', but she wasn't there. The old characters have died out now, the Welfare State has made tramping unnecessary.

Elizabeth Routledge Holmes, February 1960

Fearsome Women

Nanny Knockabout, I remember her very well. I never heard her maiden name but her married name was Carr. Her husband was hanged for murder at Liverpool. She was a fearsome looking woman. At the time…about sixty-five to seventy years ago, her headquarters were in a wood at, or near, Harker, where she had a shelter of some kind. She carried a wicked looking knife and was not slow to show it, although I had never heard of her using it. At that time a brother of her husband lived at Scaleby Hill. He had two boys who went to school at Scaleby. They were a very nice family.

Isaac P. James, February 1960

No Nits

My dad used to be gamekeeper at Newbiggin Hall and nearly sixty years ago, Nanny used to have her bed under a holly bush there. At times we used to be frightened of her. She used to swear and show her gullie. We used to run like billyho shouting 'Old Nanny Knockabout, kicks her clogs about'. Once when my sister Mary and I were coming along Cumwhinton Road, old Nanny was sitting on the roadside and she made us comb her hair and said 'I'll give you a penny for every one you find'. But we found nothing as her hair was really clean. She used to have about seven petticoats on and looked like a little barrel.

Mrs M. Hayton, February 1960

Afraid of Dogs

I remember, as a boy before the First World War, we had a maid called Janet Smith, one of the 'good old types' abounding in those days. Janet used to enthrall us as children with tales of 'Auld Nanny Knockabout', who she said swore like a trooper and was not afraid of any policemen. The only thing she was afraid of was a dog, much to the joy of the farmers who had a very real fear that she would set their barns alight; she smoked a clay cutty pipe.

H.F. Coulson, February 1960

Gullie Mary

Nanny Knockabout, or Gullie Mary as she was better known...was nice with women and children if they were civil with her. She seemed to get quite a kick out of frightening men with her gullie...a man that knew a lot about her said her people kept an hotel on the Newcastle side. When she was young she had a disappointment and she took to the roads and all men always got a rough time with Mary, but her bark was worse than her bite...no-one has ever told yet where she ended her days.

J. Bristo, March 1960

Arrested

In the barn at Little Corby Hall [the farm was unoccupied then] Nanny was secure...until one day she was disturbed by a call from the police who had been looking about. Nanny was arrested for sleeping out without any visible means of subsistence. Although Nanny walked many miles she was reluctant to walk in the company of two policemen, Sergeant Huck and PC Joseph Nanson. I was looking over the garden hedge and she sat down against a house end in Little Corby and refused to go any further. PC Nanson went to Corby Hill blacksmith's shop and requisitioned John James' pony and digby to convey her to Brampton where she received a nominal sentence of fourteen days in the cells.

John Forster, February 1960

Unwelcome Visitor

In 1902 (I was between eight and nine), I was cleaning my clogs for school at our back door, when there was three awful knocks on the front door. I was alarmed and shouted to my mother in the kitchen 'There's somebody at the front door'. Mother replied 'Well see who it is'. Now this door had a heavy bolt at the bottom and was also locked. I managed to free the bolt with a struggle and was just going to turn the key when a voice from outside boomed, 'Cum on git the door open't'. I got the door opened and had my first and last close-up of old Nanny and fled screaming, 'It's old Nanny Knockabout!' But Nanny got her breakfast and believe it or not remarked (I heard this from out of sight of course) 'Sorry if ah've freetent the bit bairn'.

William Pitts, February 1960

Hey-Fer-Lads

Edward Storey, better known as 'Hey-Fer-Lads', was perhaps more of a simpleton who did odd jobs such as 'bullock walloping' at cattle sales. In the role of 'Pussyfoot', he managed to win a prize at a fancy dress parade.

D.J. Beattie, July 1958

Jimmy Dyer

Hey-Fer-Lads (Edward Storey) in the gutter of Lowther Street, advertising Jack Dolan's hairdressers with sandwich boards.

Jimmy Dyer used to stand under Wheatley's clock in English Street about 1898 and 1899…I used to give him ½d. I have a verse…his own composition:

> 'Oh it was a gay night and day
> Fair and cloudy weather,
> Fiddle and I wondering by
> Over the world together'.

Mrs H. Wightman, November 1956

A Star Turn

Jimmy Dyer of course, was the star turn of those days, though I don't remember any boys shouting after him. He was a big, stoutish bearded man with a bulbous red nose and huge splay feet, his boots slashed across the front to relieve pressure on his corns and bunions. His clothes were shabby and he wore a flat topped bowler. His stance was in front of the gaol door where on Saturday evenings he fiddled and chanted the verses he composed. To myself, as a choirboy, his music never sounded particularly tuneful. He lived in a slum quarter off Rickergate. It was said that when he took his tatie-pot to the bakehouse to be cooked, he spat in it to make sure no-one else took it.

James Beaty, July 1958

An Imposter

Yes I knew Jimmy Dyer as they called him when I was young and it is known he was a gentleman born and he preferred his street singing and his disguise, false whiskers' for his living of course. A mystery to me as where he lived, I think nobody knew. He was a grand old fellow, but he was quite young and he sold sheets of songs which he composed himself, for 1d and I don't think there was anybody could beat him at fiddling and singing.

Mrs Farish, December 1956

Workhouse Death

I was in service with Mr and Mrs Hetherington, 33 Lonsdale Street, for eight years and sometimes Jimmy Dyer came to see Mr Hetherington and borrowed money. I think he paid his weekly lodging money and he always came and paid back when he said he would.

I remember Revd James Christie of Fisher Street church coming and leaving the message to tell Mr Hetherington Jimmy Dyer was being buried and asking Mr Hetherington to go to the funeral with him. He talked of Jimmy in the Sunday morning service. Mr Christie was chaplin [at the workhouse where Jimmy died on 16 June 1903]. I remember Mr Christie saying in his talk 'Rattle his bones over the stones, he is only a pauper who nobody owns'.

Jimmy had a sister who lived in the hotel in Keswick. I forget if she owned it or worked in it, but my auntie [at Keswick] told me he used to come. He was a great walker.

Jeanie Smith, January 1961

Blow the Fire

Street musicians were not often photographed, but Jimmy Dyer was always a showman and not camera shy. His battered bag contained the song sheets that he sold. The postmark date on this card is 1904 and the sender has written 'Gone but not Forgotten'.

Jimmy Dyer we knew very well, my friend and I being chased by him often through Warwick Street and along Corporation Road, after insulting him by calling out 'Jimmy Dyer blow the fire, hip hip hurray'. He never caught us as he couldn't run fast in such big boots and I really think he enjoyed himself. Later in life, when my friends used to meet him he was quite the gentleman and never failed to bow and raise his hat.

Mrs Ella Middleton (née Kennedy), December 1955

Monkey Green, an Italian by birth, was often seen on the streets of Carlisle with his monkey and barrel organ.

Jubilee Visit

I am no writer but could give a true and interesting experience on the occasion of Queen Victoria's Diamond Jubilee in London. I met Jimmy Dyer twice in London on this great day [in 1897] and on several times had a talk with him and a drink.

Tom Ferguson, November 1960

Best-Dressed Monkey

Monkey Green travelled further than Carlisle, as I remember him in Kirkoswald when I was a schoolgirl. His monkey had a red jacket and bright green trousers, very tame and a great delight to us children. The monkey collected the pennies to put in a mug.

Mrs B.A. Simpson, August 1968

Clog Dancing

When I was a little girl, not very old, as soon as I saw Monkey Green coming I used to run home and shout 'Here's the organ man and his monkey' and I asked for ½d and my dad always gave me a penny. Myself and all my girl friends danced on the flags…all us girls in them days wore clogs.

Mrs C. McSkimming, May 1964

Street Entertainment

Directly opposite my grandmother's house [in Jane Street] lived Monkey Green, who lived with his married daughter and her husband. He went out daily with his barrel organ and monkey and returned each evening. There were quite a few street entertainers in this day [the 1920s]. There were two men who often came around with a barrel organ, sometimes with their faces blackened. One had the dummy of a woman, whose feet he attached to his own with straps and holding the dummy around the waist, he would dance around the street, to music supplied by his friend with the hand organ.

There was a good selection of street musicians and singers who often came around and after a few minutes performance would make a door to door collection. There was also a man with a mobile children's roundabout who often came around. This was mounted on a four-wheeled cart with small wheels and pulled by a horse. It was operated by turning a mangle-type wheel with a handle on. A ride on it cost a penny, or indeed a handful of rags if you had no money.

D. Laing, May 1976

Jimmy the Fiddler

Jimmy the fiddler I shall never forget, not so much for his street activities, but for the fact that for many months of each year, when I was a small boy, he lived in his caravan in an old lane close to my home [at Todhills] and was a friend of the family. At that time his

Jimmy the fiddler was never without his dog, but this did not prevent people from mistaking him in their memory for Jimmy Dyer.

companion, Maggie, was a small slight old lady, who used to help the family income by street singing in various parts of the city.

But the day I shall never forget was when it became necessary to move the canvas top of his caravan to a new wagon. To do this he had enlisted the help of a few young lads from Todhills, to lift and carry the top over to the new wagon standing alongside. The number of strange and unmentionable items that came tumbling out when the old top was lifted defy description and the scene with the old pair fussing about amongst it will always be remembered. However, all ended well and late in the afternoon, the top firmly fixed on the new wagon, Jimmy, well refreshed, seated himself upon the wagon front with his fiddle and gladly gave an hour's rendering of all the old airs.

To add to the entertainment, a well-known chap from Todhills selected two long willows from a nearby bush and gave a memorable display of the 'sword dance', local style. It was a wonderful day and at night a new van was ready for the road. 'James Williamson, Musician, Workington' was marked on the flyboard, with the retriever Robbie and the collie Rob Roy tied up and asleep underneath.

The last time I saw Jimmy was years after this, sitting playing under the arch near the courts, English Street and I could hardly say he looked any different.

Edward McBurnie, November 1956

Sister Lillie

The line to Silloth branched off the Edinburgh line and as the Silloth trains steamed slowly round the curve [at Willow Holme], we had plenty of time to watch the large numbers of people who waved from the carriage windows. There were also many train loads of children who were taken down to Silloth by Sister Lillie, a very well known philanthropist.

D. Laing, March 1976

Pied Piper

In the *Cumberland News* my friend had marked the reference 'Pied Piper'

which referred to my work. It was such a surprise. It recalled my entrance to the city in 1917 to be a social worker, to face facts. Then thro' the years to witness the great improvements being made – today life has less strain – truly equalised. I was touched to have been remembered by the Press and how much the *Cumberland News* helped our work and their keen interest of the children going to Silloth and the erection of the shelter. So much owing to Mrs Harrison, our fairy godmother. My retirement since 1937 has been in the [south of] England.

Sister Lillie Davis, MBE, December 1955

An Unexpected Holiday

We were very poor and lived in Hope's Court, Port Road, when to my mother's surprise a ticket was handed to her to go to Silloth the following Saturday. It was given by Mrs Malloy, a lady who worked in Carr's Biscuit Factory and her friend Miss Allen.

They were two ordinary girl workers and collected coppers from their fellow worker's in Carr's and were able to take ten or more children to Silloth each Saturday. These two girls have never had any tributes paid to them for giving us such a happy time at the seaside. There was the Sister Lillie Shelter those days, but we were taken to the cocoa rooms and given a mug of tea and a bag of cakes and two pennies each to spend which we did like millionaires.

Mrs M. Swindle, December 1955

CHAPTER 3

Getting about

A busy day on English Street in 1933. Two buses set off southwards from the Town Hall.

Staff at Langholm Station stand on the single platform with the stationmaster in the centre. Langholm was at the terminus of a branch from Riddings Junction on the Waverley line.

First Trip To Carlisle

Langholm Station in those days [1910] was a station to be proud of, having a stationmaster, clerk, two porters, two signalmen, two engine drivers and firemen, as well as others employed in the goods yard. I well remember my first journey to Carlisle and in those days it was quite a thrill. Tickets were bought, examined and checked. The guard tested the brakes and walked along the platform with his flags under his arm; a word to the driver, a last look at his watch, then waving the green flag, the driver replying with a shrill blast from the engine, and we were on our way. The excitement was mounting, we were on our way to Carlisle, a city with a large railway station and for the first time in my life I would see the main line and the express trains.

What stories had been told about these monsters; how dangerous it was to stand too near the edge of the platform. People had been drawn in by the thunderous roar and rush as they sped onwards to the large cities.

How neat and tidy the little stations looked; the number of people travelling; the importance and hustle and bustle of those days. The greatest moment came as we drew near to Carlisle Station; not two lines, but dozens, signals too numerous to mention; goods trains moving in different directions; tank engines busy shunting. But more interesting was the different colours of the engines: Caledonian blue; Midland green and North British bronze green. They were beautifully kept, especially the passenger locomotives for the main line.

Arriving at the station was a moment I will always remember. The tremendous sound of trains, the hissing of high pressure steam, the clang of the metal coupling rods as the wheels spun and engines straining under heavy loads. Milk cans being shifted, porter's barrows being pushed along the platforms and a general noise of trains arriving and departing. The thunderous blast from the engines exhaust and people rushing about for their train. All this in the age of the rocket, diesel and jet propulsion, may seem a bit far fetched to the modern youth, but to me from the quiet town of Langholm it will be a day I will always remember.

Andrew Irving, December 1962

Cabs

I very well remember Court Square with its hansom cabs. The building in the middle of the square did not follow the advent of the car, but was built as a cabstand while hansom cabs still were in use. I well remember when it was built [in 1905]. The cabstand later became a taxi stand and which, incidentally, I trust has been completely removed since my last visit

The hustle and bustle of activity on Carlisle Station platform at the time that Andrew Irving described it.

two years ago, at which time it was in a terrible state of dilapidation.

Stan Goldsworthy, December 1959 and 6 June 1970

A Grand Day Out

Ibought a second-hand bicycle from a young fellow in Carr's office which… cost me the large sum of 18s 9d! This was from an advertisement I had seen in the *Cumberland News*. At the age of sixteen, with one of my pals, Joe Radford, we set off for a run and arrived at Annan. We explored the town and having a few coppers each, bought ourselves some biscuits and lemonade and eventually rode to the [Shawhill] station there.

It so happened that a train was about due and as this was making for Bowness across the Solway, by the viaduct, we had the bright idea of boarding it, so we bought tickets which I think were 2 ½d each. The train arrived and we deposited the bikes in the luggage van and duly arrived at Bowness Station. We mounted again and cycled from there to the village. By chance we met a party which had travelled for an outing in a horse-drawn charabanc from Carlisle. They had arranged to have tea in the village hall and they kindly invited us to join them. Didn't we enjoy the Solway salmon!

It ended with the journey on our cycles via Port Carlisle, Drumburgh and across Burgh Marsh – at this time the road had a very rough surface of clay and lots of loose stones, also potholes galore. We arrived home in Carlisle after a most enjoyable day's excursion

Bowness Station in 1913, about the date that Wilf Welsh arrived there after travelling over the Solway Viaduct from Annan.

The Solway Viaduct survived after damage by ice flows in 1881 and was re-opened in 1883. It was closed for war economy measures between 1916 and 1919. This photograph is thought to show the last train over the viaduct in 1921. Until demolition in 1934-35, it remained as a hazardous, unofficial footpath from Scotland to England – used especially on Sundays when pubs in Scotland were closed.

and feeling better with the exercise and sunshine.

Wilf Welsh, May 1976

Solway Viaduct

In my younger days I enjoyed the journey by train over the viaduct across Solway's stormy waters. Incidentally, a party of us crossed the viaduct when rail traffic ceased and it meant a rather perilous walk for we had to jump over the gaping holes, caused through neglect and decay. Needless to say we did not attempt the journey again.

Ben McCubbin, November 1965

Walking the Bridge

I can remember as a boy being given the weekly job of 'walking the bridge' every Saturday morning, carrying the money to Jack Holmes to pay for salmon delivered [to my father's fishmonger shop] during the previous week. The railway service had been discontinued by this time and the fish were brought by boat and picked up at Seafield.

A.T. McGlasson, May 1975

Dandy Coaches

There were two, known as the 'little dandy' and the 'big dandy'. The two ran together to Drumburgh Junction on busy occasions and the bigger one

47

was driven by the stationmaster. Port Carlisle in my early days was quite a little holiday resort for Carlisle families and the cottages and houses were let by the local residents. Some visitors stayed at Dands Temperance Hotel in the village.

Many years ago a list used to appear in the *Cumberland News* during the summer months of the visitors and families from Carlisle. So much have times changed, a holiday at Port Carlisle would not be very much appreciated in these days.

Wilf Welsh, November 1971

Horse Drawn Railway

I remember the Dandy coach very well. Over fifty years ago my father's uncle had a farm at Glasson and I often went there. Every Saturday his daughter came to Carlisle to do the shopping. I came with her on the Dandy. I thought it was great being pulled by horses on the railway line.

Miss M.A. Armstrong, November 1960

A Solway Storm

My sister and I (fourteen and sixteen years respectively) lived at Anthorn and on the morning of the 3 September 1902 we set off to Kirkbride to see a friend of my mother to the train for Carlisle. We had to cross Whitrigg Marsh and across a humped bridge over the River Wampool. The gale was so strong we could hardly keep on our feet. Having seen our friend off the next thing was to get back home and we were told the tide was coming in fast

The 'little dandy' arrives at Port Carlisle, having come from Drumburgh Junction through Glasson. The date is between 1908 and 1912.

A family from Carlisle are pictured outside the house at Port Carlisle that they had taken for the summer.

and was all around the base of the said bridge. It was terrifying to see the water rushing under the bridge and when we got over the water was level with the embankment. It was dreadful to walk on the sleepers with the wind lashing at us and the water swirling each side.

Two postman who lived on the Whitrigg [side] were returning after their rounds, followed close behind us and said afterwards that they were surprised that two girls managed to get to Whitrigg Station as it took them all they had got to do it. The stationmaster and his wife (Mr and Mrs Henderson) were anxiously watching us and many times we were hidden from them by the spray. We got to Whitrigg Station, soaking and exhausted and were put to bed in the station house while our clothes were dried by Mrs Henderson.

We set off in the evening and our parents came to meet us. They had been anxious about us. It was a very dangerous and risky thing to cross by the railway, as just afterwards it was completely submerged.

Mrs Mary Lenton (née Marshall), March 1957

The Crash

There was Reay's Millhouse Farm [in Willow Holme]…I was watching the horses being harnessed in the farmyard; the quiet was shattered by something which I still remember vividly. There was a rending, splintering, crash and the deep thud shook the ground. Someone shouted that it was the railway and the few of us that were around dashed over the farmyard and around behind the farmhouse. There, over on the curve, our eyes met a terrible sight. A train of some half a dozen carriages, coming into Carlisle, had crashed!

Being too young [ten] to appreciate the real gravity of the situation, our impulse was to have a closer look, so we immediately set off running and were at the railway embankment in no time flat. We scrambled through a hole in the hedge and hurried up the bank. The first two or three coaches had partly telescoped, the others derailed. The engine lay in a huge hole in the

ground and there was smoke and steam everywhere and a lot of shouting. There were suitcases, tablecloths, crockery and spoons scattered all over the place. We weren't allowed to linger long, however, because suddenly shouting figures in football strip and others in Army uniform were running about and we were chased away.

I learned later that they were Army personnel, who had been playing a match on the nearby football pitch on the Sheepmount, owned by the Border Regiment. The tenants of Barwise Nook were later to tear up sheets and other linen for bandages for the injured and I remember my mother making a

On 3 January 1931 a train travelling to Carlisle from Hawick took the Willow Holme curve at over 40mph when it should have been travelling at 15mph. The resulting crash left the locomotive *Northumberland* deeply buried in the embankment.

The farmyard at Willow Holme where D. Laing was playing when he heard the crash.

large jug of tea which was sent across. I think there were three killed and forty injured.

…That night was lit up by flares and overlights, the breakdown men working all night. When the engine was lifted, it was placed on a nearby siding and, swathed in tarpaulins, was roped and sealed before removal.

D. Laing, March 1976

The Silloth Line

I was the first and at that time the only schoolboy to travel daily to the grammar school from Silloth. Selkirk, the bearded guard looked out for any of us laggards and held the early morning train for we regulars, who included the Leach sisters, an architect, John Cotteral (the schoolmaster) and a young man who worked in a Carlisle drapers. We reached Abbey Town, the station name being sonorously called by the stationmaster, where a solicitor joined us. The later comers lost their status with us as we neared Carlisle. One or two at Drumburgh, from Port Carlisle via the 'Dandy'; young Jessamine at Burgh, with a bright little bullet-headed boy, Bobby Calvert, who was immediately lifted unresistingly to travel on the luggage rack to Carlisle. The name Lt Robert Calvert appears on the local First World War memorial. We were still in the days of the flat tins for boiling water in each carriage, the only heating we had.

Through the Mozart Wilson family leaving their weekly copy of *The Stage* behind them in the carriage, when they changed at Abbey Junction for Aspatria ('lowp oot') after one of their summer seasons at Silloth, I became interested in the theatre world, where I have spent my lifetime.

There is the inevitable nostalgic twinge at the Silloth line's closing, but it had lost some of its character with the closing of some of the stations and the ripe personalities *en route*.

A.C. Astor (one time manager of HM Theatre, Carlisle), 1964

A Slow Journey

I had travelled by a painfully slow train from Bullgill to Brigham Junction. Ancient Lancashire and Yorkshire carriages, with severe horse-hair seats and obsolete gas lamps, headed by an old LNWR tank engine, made up that comical train, which crawled along at 15mph. I thought we were being stuck all day at Dearham and Papcastle Stations! Nobody seemed to be in any hurry. Somewhere along the train I could hear poultry squawking and some child having his (or her) bottom smacked. The scene was such as one could have expected in Ireland. At my destination I commented to the driver about the slow journey. He laughingly said, 'Aye lad! Ah call me injun "Tortoise" – an' we hev another called "Snail"! Can ta beat that?'

Tom Jackson

Wagonettes

How many people remember Young's wagonettes? How well I remember them…they were 'stabled' behind Garfield Street, which meant that all the residents of the street had full view from their upper storey of the yard where all the stables were and where all the wagonettes – huge vehicles as they were – were kept. As a quite young boy it was most interesting to look from our rear bedroom window at the activities across the way, including the movements of the wagonettes and the arrival and unloading of vast quantities of fodder for the fine horses.

Stan Goldsworthy, June 1970

One of Young's wagonettes from a company billhead.

Post Office Houghton.

Thomas Bell, a rural postman better known as 'Tommy the Post', called at Houghton post office on his outward journey from Carlisle.

Tommy The Post

I well remember as a very small child accompanied by my older sister, walking from our home in the Dalston Road area to Eden Bridge, where we waited for 'Tommy the Post' and his pony and trap. At that time we had relatives farming near Smithfield and we spent frequent holidays there.

We used to join Tommy (I never remember hearing his surname) at around 5.30 to 6 a.m. and very chilly it often was at that early hour. Tommy had an old grey pony and we trotted along at a very leisurely pace. What happy journeys those were. His trap was a small round tub-shaped vehicle with a door in the back and there was room inside for Tommy, his mail and our two selves. There were in those days no buses and no tarmac roads and no

rubber-tyred wheels on our vehicle! We were sometimes allowed to drive and felt very important, thought the pony knew every step of the way and needed no help from us.

Tommy's daily journey took him as far as Kirklinton delivering and collecting mail and parcels on the way and our first call was at Houghton post office. We called at houses and farms by the wayside and if the house was a little distant from the roadside, Tommy blew a blast on his whistle which brought the housewife running for her mail. Sometimes we made a detour to some outlying farm. At Smithfield we said goodbye to Tommy and from there we walked on a rough cart road across two fields to our destination, Brownrigg. When our holiday came to an end, we met Tommy again at Smithfield for the return journey. If my memory serves

53

me, we took a different route on the return and I seem to remember coming through Scaleby. When our friends left the district our trips with Tommy came to an end. By that time he was well on in years and very lame and I think he probably retired…soon after that. Tommy was a gruff old chap with a shock of curly white hair and a white beard, but he was never anything but kind and courteous and there was always a bag of sweeties in his pocket for us. I often still think of Tommy and I shall always remember those journeys with pleasure.

Hilda Brown, August 1969

Minding the Pony

Tommy the Post (Thomas Bell) brings back happy memories. As a boy I used to meet Tom between the Near Boot and Far Boot. I was allowed to ride on the back step of the trap into Carlisle. Then I watched the pony till he delivered his mail bags to the post office, the back premises then being in Crosby Street. Then he would let me drive the pony to the stables in West Tower Street. I was paid the handsome sum of one penny.

T.H. Elliot, August 1969

Mews

Reference to horse-drawn traffic recalls a place in Carlisle which I have never seen any mention of…this being the famous 'posh' [County] Mews on the east side of Lowther Street, where the well-to-do farmers and other country residents stabled their horses and parked their vehicles while in the city.

Stan Goldsworthy, July 1974

Bicycles

J.S. Farrer, photographer of Brampton and Wetheral, was my father. He was born in 1860 and died in 1952. He would own one of the first bicycles in Cumberland and he cycled to his photographers business in Brampton, three days every week for over thirty years.

Mrs F.M. Irving, October 1961

Making Bikes

One cyclist was a man who built cycles from parts which he cannibalised from old machines. Once he had one rebuilt, he would ride down 'The Holme' [Willow Holme] with a large box of tools on the back. When a bike was not running right, he would dismount and start making some adjustments. It was not uncommon to see him using a hammer!

D. Laing, May 1976

Lighting up Time

Yes Willow Holme at night could be very eerie. An ideal setting, I often think, for a Boris Karloff film. At night there was no vehicles, only

A Carlisle cycling club has ventured into Scotland, not far from Lochmaben.

an occasional cyclist. It was about this time that I acquired my first bike. It was an ancient machine of obscure vintage and had what was supposed to be a back pedalling brake. The theory was that by pedalling in a reverse direction, the brake acted on the hub of the rear wheel, but alas, this never worked satisfactorily. The front tyre was torn and needed replacement. This I effected by purchasing a second-hand tyre at a cycle shop in Abbey Street for a shilling and after repairing the puncture in the inner tube was mobile. The bike had cost me two shillings and sixpence all told.

I had an oil lamp which was much in use those days to provide my light at night. I also had a carbide lamp which my older brother discarded. In construction it was a small container (holding the carbide) with a small water tank on top. A tube led from the lower container (holding the carbide) to a lamphouse in front. By regulating a knob on top, the water was allowed to drip into the carbide thus producing a gas which then went through the tube into the lamphouse. By lighting the gas burner, a steady white light was obtained. But constant leakage obliged me to scrap it.

D. Laing, May 1976

Mobile Doctors

Doctors in those days [1895] had no cars. Some of them rode bicycles. Two of the best loved doctors in Carlisle were Dr Norman McLaran and his father. Dr Norman was a fine looking man, 6 feet tall and weighed around 175 lbs. He thought nothing of walking from Portland Square to the infirmary and back to his office.

The elder doctor McLaran was one of nature's gentlemen. Money to a lot of doctors in those days was only a secondary consideration. They were doctors first and always.

Richard Carruthers, March 1959

Women Cyclists

The Border City Wheeler 100 mile trial [in 1933] interested me because I was there and won a certificate. Miss Jessie Blakeney and myself both clocked 8 hours 52 minutes. We went round within the men's scheduled time, while three of the stronger sex retired and one was outside the allowed time. The route was from Carlisle to Penrith, over Shap Fell to Kendal for lunch; Kendal via Staveley and Windemere, over Dunmail Raise to Threlkeld for tea and then through Troutbeck, Greystoke and Hutton End, finishing at the grandstand of Carlisle Racecourse.

Mrs D. Birkett (Dot Foster), 1975

Sociable Bike

Near Fendley's shop, a cycle manufacturer called Fred Pickering brought out what he called a 'Sociable' safety bike in about 1896. You sat side by side. His apprentice and yours truly often had a ride around town to advertise it, but I don't think it became popular. I had an electric light on my own bike then, off a small wet cell. I charged it up off a dynamo. I have lots of pleasant memories of Carlisle such as Hannah Baty's 'taffie'.

Tom Graham, February 1959

Bicycle Made For Two

I remember seeing that bike being ridden by two persons going up London Road towards Harraby. A short time later it came back down with only one on it and he stopped to talk to a friend. I was standing in the doorway of Rutherford's draper's shop across from Alexander Street.

I crossed the street to see the bike and the friend got on and the two rode away. This was a Sunday afternoon. I understand from the conversation that it was made in the bike shop.

James P. Brodie

Trams

A very interesting event...had to do with the first tram to serve the Denton Holme district [in 1900]. It seems there had been a miscalculation as to the extent of the clearance under the railway bridge on Denton Street.

The Denton Street railway bridge with a tram underneath on the first day of running, 29 June 1900. It looks as though the tram might be stuck there. Stan Goldsworthy is possibly one of the boys looking on.

When the tram proceeded to pass under the bridge with its trolley down flush with the roof, it was discovered it would not pass under and it jammed quite tightly under the bridge. It was a long time before it was possible to extricate it. This was a thrilling sight for us boys.

Stan Goldsworthy, December 1959

Tramway Closure

In 1931 [when the tramway closed], during a procession, a coster boy complete with barrow, laden with rags and scrap metal, departed from Carlisle Castle decorated with balloons etc and the useful slogan 'Tram cars for rags – points for Carlisle'. Carlisle United were then in very low water.

Simon Keiling, May 1962

Motor Cars

I was very much interested in…Jim Fendley's shop on Cecil Street… and his cars. I remember my dad coming home and saying, 'They have got a machine now that runs without horses.' A few days after that, Jim went through Carleton with his car (I lived at Carleton) and asked me to have a ride, which I did. He went as far as Upperby and then brought me home. That must have been sixty or sixty-five years ago

[1896]. I am seventy-seven now…When I got a little older I bought a three-speed [motor] bicycle off him for £10. I was over in 1950 and passed where his shop used to be. After being away from that part for forty years I saw some great changes.

William Wood, April 1959

Car Hire

I have good reason to remember the car AO 421, as it was the only one in the cortege at my father's funeral sixty-three years ago, from Low Moorhouse to Burgh-by-Sands churchyard. Motors were few and far between in those days. The owner at that time was James Little of Botcherby Grange, who had his business premises as joiner and undertaker in Caldewgate. Mr Little's

wife was my cousin.

Mrs J.A. Johnstone, September 1970

Woman Driver

Mrs E.L. Crowther, who claimed to be the first lady motorist in Carlisle in 1905, owned and used an Invalid Motor Chair in 1945. This enabled her to get around and out for runs. She also used it when attending the Carlisle Music Festivals. The first owner of this invalid chair was F. McMorran, Cotehill. It was the first of its kind in Cumberland.

M. Hill, October 1970

Jim Fendley's works viewed from Cecil Street, where he made a steam car in 1896.

Emilie Crowther had been the first lady driver in Carlisle to own a car in 1905. This invalid motor chair was run by her in the late 1940s and early '50s.

Dusty Roads

Joseph Bell, the County Surveyor, about 1902 gave his views on modern motoring, which he considered to be rather a menace to the roads. He thought cars should have solid tyres and not travel above 15mph to avoid a dust hazard.

Helen Graham, October 1970

Stranded

Sir Alexander B.W. Kennedy, MIMechE, secured the contract for erecting the generating station for the Corporation of Carlisle and my father was appointed resident engineer in 1898. On the completion of the contract, he was invited by the Corporation to become the city electrical engineer. He accepted the appointment early in 1899.
I am not sure of the facts but believe my father…[made a car] operated by batteries. I seem to remember the story

On Monday 12 May 1919, a converted Handley Page bomber, which was dropping *Daily Mail* newspapers by parachute at Carlisle, made an emergency landing at Harker. It had been in difficulties and was repaired on the ground, but crashed on take off.

of getting stranded and daddy spending all day underneath it putting it right!

F.C.S. Burnet, September 1971

these planes stopped on the Swifts at Carlisle.

Jas Maxwell, 1957

Harker Crash

Now at Harker a plane was forced down in a field. It was the *Daily Mail* plane that dropped newspapers on the Swifts at Carlisle. Thousands came to see this. It was made mostly of wood [and canvas]. It was repaired [there] and when they tried to take off it crashed into a hedge, knocked its wheels off and was smashed to pieces. The pilot was injured and taken to the infirmary.

I remember being on Rockcliffe Marsh with my grandmother to see aeroplanes in the first 'Round Britain Air Race' going over...I believe one of

Rooftop Vigil

Sydney Swann was not only, among other things, a gifted parson, a famous oarsman, a good cricketer and a pilot capable of making his own aeroplane as well as flying it, but he was a considerable architect. He planned and built his own vicarage in Northumberland Road [now Victoria Place], known as Wyvern, when he went to the new parish of St Aidan's.

Whether it was prescience on his part or not I do not know, but one of the features of his house...is a flat roof arranged in two terraces, the lower with a wooden railing at the edge.

There was nothing more pleasant on a summery day than to sit on a deck chair on the roof and view the Swifts, Stanwix and the river. It was a perfect grandstand for the Round Britain Air Race [in 1911]…for me and my brothers it was one of our greatest events; we stayed on the roof night and day and missed nothing; the airmen in those days rose little higher than our heads as we stood on the roof. They passed directly above us coming up from the Swifts; we saw their faces clearly and they all waved to us. I think the names of the Frenchmen…[included] Gustav Hamel.

You may imagine my delight when about a year ago the present residents allowed me to go over our old home and, once again, on the roof where I noted the chimney stack on which we carved a record of so historic an occasion in the development of flying.

R.F. Millard, February 1958

A Flying Vicar

My father, the Revd S. Swann…was a very unusual man. He did ride from Carlisle to London on a Dursley Pedersen bicycle, finding his way and getting his food as best he could. It was a single-geared machine, which was all that was available in those days and therefore not ideal for bicycling up Shap and coming down. When he went to Crosby Ravensworth [as vicar]… he started on making an aeroplane [in 1908]. One day we would have the tail behind and then on the next day decide to try it in front. The machine was a wonderful contraption of bamboo poles braced together with wire and unfortunately the Arrol Johnson engine which he obtained was too heavy for the power which it developed and so it was extremely difficult to get the thing into the air, especially as my father weighed nearly 14 stone. But into the air it did get, but thank God, not far;

One of the aircraft which landed on the Swifts in the Round Britain Air Race on 25 July 1911.

when eventually he came down in a flock of sheep he thought it was time to call it a day.

Canon S.E. Swann, January 1958

Buses

J.J. Wallis of Beaconsfield Street started his bus service between the Town Hall and Wetheral on Saturday 4 August 1923. He ran every hour daily at a single fare of 6d to Wetheral and 4d to Scotby and was, I believe, the pioneer on the route, certainly as far as a daily service was concerned.

Early in 1929 the LNER, who since January of that year had controlled Robert Emmerson & Co. (who ran the Carlisle-Newcastle service) applied for licenses…to run between Carlisle and Wetheral. Despite opposition by Mrs Wallis, who claimed she was losing money on the service, permission was granted. Emmerson started their service on Whit Monday 1929. This was too much for Mrs Wallis who sold out to Emmerson in July 1929, who in turn went to United in February 1930, who then took over Fidler's service as well in January 1934.

Mr Wallis started his service with a 28-seat Karrier bus HH 1919 and added a second vehicle, a 14-seater Austro Fiat HH 2130, in November 1923. This service was continued by Mr Wallis' widow after his death in September 1925 and in 1926 she added two further vehicles (one replacing the Karrier), Albions seating 24 and 29, HH 2992 and HH 3251. The service was advertised as the Green and White Bus Co., but the livery was later changed (I

don't know when) to chocolate with a red band.

In June 1928 a third Albion (32-seater HH 4363) was acquired in place of the Austro Fiat and was necessary as a competitor had started at this time on the route, Mr A.J. Fidler, who was, I think, associated with Richard Percival Ltd, who in turn was controlled by the Balfour Beatty Group who also owned the city tramways.

Richard Percival was the real pioneer in Carlisle, prior to his takeover in 1922.

David A. Grisenthwaite, July 1973

Colourful Buses

The bus service to Langholm was supplied by Messrs Hudson of Caldewgate, who were also in business as funeral furnishers. Other bus firms, of which there were quite a few, operated then [late 1920s] in Carlisle. Names like Percivals Motor Services, White Star Motor Services, Adairs Bus Company and Hodgsons, to name but a few. Hodgson's ran orange coloured 'Beardmore' buses which had oval-shaped brass radiators. They plied between Carlisle and Port Carlisle and Bowness. They were to be seen on Saturdays bringing in country people to the market with baskets of butter and eggs packed on the roof. This was surrounded by an iron rail about a foot high and a little ladder fixed on the rear of the bus allowed access to the top, where the baskets were passed to be secured. It was customary for lads of those days to meet these vehicles at the Town Hall and offer to carry the individual baskets to the market in

A Wallis bus heads off along Warwick Road in the mid-1920s on its way to Wetheral.

The Carlisle & Dalston District Bus Service bus, operated by Mr J. Wharton of Dalston, awaits passengers at the Town Hall, Carlisle.

exchange for a tip.

Another rather colourful bus was that of the Longtown-based Lochinvar Bus Company. These buses were maroon with a red tartan stripe painted midway around the body. The local depot was in the Pigg Market, at the bottom of Corporation Road. I believe they were eventually taken over by the Caledonian which in turn was swallowed by the Western SMT. Most of the others succumbed to the Ribble [in 1930]. These were the times of the one penny ride from the Town Hall to Raffles.

D. Laing, May 1976

Gretna Bus

There was no bus service [through Todhills] when the War ended. Tom Graham of Gretna started to run a few passengers to Carlisle. His bus was very simple, like a van with seats up each side, door at the back and no side windows. It would hold about twelve people. He would be the pioneer of this route.

Jas Maxwell, 1957

Bus Shelters

Today, mingling with the roar of modern traffic in the heart of the city, is the penetrating noise of the pneumatic drill tearing up unsightly bus shelters, dotted about this ancient square, whose cast-iron roots are firmly embedded in concrete. The removal of these eyesores gives a more pleasing picture of the historic spot of our ancient city. No one would desire that the public should be deprived of shelter, but as has been suggested, buses should be re-routed and the stops at the Town Hall removed elsewhere, where shelters could be erected without spoiling the beauty of the city centre.

David J. Beattie, 1958

Narrow Roads

Willow Holme was only wide enough for one vehicle. These were the days [1920s] of the Model T Ford and the Sentinel Steam Lorry, one of the latter, owned by McGillivray's of Carlisle, being a regular visitor on its journey to the power station. When one of these vehicles met another coming in the opposite direction, the one nearest to a gateway had to edge into it and let the other pass. A cyclist had to dismount and get on the pavement out of the way.

D.Laing, May 1976

CHAPTER 4

War

Troops march from the castle on church parade.

Sunday Parades

Many a Sunday morning have I walked from my home in Currock to the castle to witness the church parade. This was no affair in khaki battledress, berets blue and anklets web, but was a spectacular affair of scarlet tunics, shining helmets and clanking swords. The depot was usually well manned in those days, for in addition to the regular recruits, there was also a contingent of Special Reserves under training.

The band took up their position in the centre of the square and to the tune of the *Christ Church Chimes*, the CO, wearing a white toupee, made his inspection of the parade. Then off

they would march to the cathedral. On occasions there would be a combined parade of Territorial units. This was a sight to be remembered. The Cumberland Artillery, in their blue, scarlet and gold, led the way, followed by the 4th Borders in their scarlet tunics faced with yellow. They were accompanied by their own band under the direction of that well known and accomplished bandmaster, Felix Burns.

If I remember rightly, the Yeomanry – whose dress of scarlet Eton jackets trimmed with silver braid, with a double white stripe down the trousers was as elaborate as that of many regular cavalry units – made their way to the cathedral. Such pageantry passed away with the outbreak of the

Church parade for the 1st Cumberland Artillery Volunteers in 1904. They are marching with the band in front of the Drill Hall on Strand Road along Albert Street and into Victoria Place on their way to the cathedral.

The Cumberland Militia going off to camp by train approach the Citadel Station through the Courts, c. 1901.

1914 war and is not likely to be seen in the city again.

Tom Lightfoot, May 1956

Boer War

The most exciting and never to be forgotten procession (not planned as such) was when the Border Regiment went off to the Boer War, marching through Castle Street and English Street, through thousands of spectators and in the midnight hours. It was tremendously exciting led by the band. The red tunics and white helmets and white belts made a colourful show. Wives and sweethearts hung onto the men in the other ranks and with the prevalent war fever everyone seemed to be stirred to concert pitch. The gates of the station were closed to the general public but we boys knew a way in there, which we found crowded.

James Beaty, July 1958

With the Flag to Pretoria

As a member of the 1st Volunteer Border Regiment at that time, I along with other Carlisle boys volunteered for service. During our training of six weeks we were all billeted out at various public houses, mine being the Drove Inn, which was situated at the bottom of Rickergate on the site now occupied by the [Civic Centre]. I well remember on leaving Carlisle Castle at midnight being surrounded by cheering crowds. Headed by the band and the fire brigade, who were paying a

The Lonsdale Battalion of the Border Regiment train on Carlisle Racecourse at Blackwell in 1914. On 1 July 1916 – the first day of the Battle of the Somme – 25 officers and 500 men were either killed or wounded out of a total of 28 officers and 800 other ranks.

farewell to Sergeant Billy Marshall and myself who were members of the fire brigade, they carrying flaming torches added to the wonderful send off which we had.

On reaching the Viaduct, the band, still playing and the crowd cheering, went straight on towards the station, when Major Thompson of Kendal, who was in charge gave the order to right wheel to the Viaduct entrance [to the station]. When the crowd found out their mistake, there was a general mad rush which became so thick one just had to stand still and be pushed on. The Carlisle contingent were given a flag which had to be signed by any of them that reached Pretoria. I had the honour of signing it along with others. Of the Carlisle ones who went out there only three are left, Billy Morley (Drum Major), Billy Steel and myself.

W.J. Harris, July 1958

The Lonsdales

Good luck to the Lonsdale Battal'n,
success to the boys in grey.
The counties are proud of their heroes,
And proudly they'll cheer them away,
A rousing send off they'll give them,
Though eyes will be moist and damp,
As they bid goodbye to the heroic boys,
From dear old Blackhall Camp.
[Last verse of the *Lonsdale Battalion* song written by H. Burgess, Carlisle.]

T. Gill, Durdar.

The Yeomanry

I was eighteen years of age when I joined the Westmorland & Cumberland Yeomanry on 24 November 1908 for five years, ending up as a NCO. I rejoined again on 12 September 1914, then early in 1915 out to France.

Before the 1914 war we had four squadrons of the W&C Yeomanry; A Squadron, Kendal and District; B Penrith; C Whitehaven and D Carlisle. We spent fifteen happy days at camp every year mostly at Lowther Park and we went by road, mounted. We hired our horses from the cab owners, Mr D. Crosby, West Walls; Mr D.P. Huntington of City Mews, Heads Lane and Mr J. Graham of Lowther Street, now the Ribble bus station. Early in 1917 while still in France I was transferred to a new unit along with others called the Mounted Traffic Control Squadron consisting of four troops to control traffic in the forward area.

Then later on in 1917 the Yeomanry were dismounted and transferred to the 7th Border Regiment. I finished up after the war ended in the Army of Occupation Yeomanry on 19 July 1919.

B.B. Murray, July 1958

An End to Soldiering

I continued to serve with the W&C Yeomanry from 1906 'til the time they were dismounted, August 1917. The regiment went to serve with the 7th Border Regiment. Passcendaele Ridge was our first scrap with the Borders. I was awarded the Military Medal, 10 October 1917. I went from there to Cambraie and in October 1918 I was severely wounded, losing my right arm and a severe gunshot-wound right thigh. This finished my soldiering.

Ex Sergeant William Sowerby MM, June 1958

Boy Soldiers

I was one of the boy soldiers, joining the army in 1915 at the age of fifteen by stating the wrong age and on active service four months later…Those that survived…were sent home at the back end of 1916 and re-formed in a battalion of the Royal Scots.

W.H. Eldridge, October 1965

Too Old

My own age on joining up and sent to Aldershot, was forty-three and [I was] told I could be more useful on the south coast alive (perhaps), than dead, when the roses were blooming in Picardy.

R. Baxter, October 1958

The Gretna Disaster

At the time of the great Gretna disaster, I was serving in the Royal Army Medical Corps and just previous to the disaster had been posted to the Chadwick Hospital for temporary duty.

The result was that I spent the whole of that terrible Saturday at the scene. Later I spent some three years in France, mainly on the Somme, and I can safely say that there I came across nothing so terrible. I wonder how many of the old Chadwick staff are still in the Carlisle district?

C. Skelton, October 1955

The Quintinshill disaster, which occurred near Gretna on 22 May 1915, was the worst railway crash in this country, with the largest loss of life. Because the accident happened during the war and due to the fact that most of the casualties were soldiers, it did not have the impact that it would have done during peacetime. Many of those who died were trapped in the burning wreckage. Onlookers, many on bicycles and some from as far away as Carlisle, watched the recovery work.

Worst Disaster

Out of a grand total 227 killed and 247 injured, approximately 200 dead belonged to the 7th Royal Scots Regiment, mainly from Edinburgh and Leith. The driver and fireman of the troop train were both killed. They belonged to Carlisle, the driver Frank Scott who lived at Etterby. The fireman was James Hannah who also lived at Etterby. David Wallace, Andrew Johnston and John Cooper, all belonged to Carlisle, the crews of the other engines involved in the crash were all injured.

My father, who was a sergeant in the Border Regiment, arrived on an earlier train on leave from France that dreadful Whit Saturday.

Simon Keiling, July 1974

Arrival of Injured

Robert Hogg, of the City Museum, told me how he watched the injured arrive [in the city] as a small boy of four and a half.

J.A.B. Hamilton, December 1968

Treating the Injured

My eldest brother, who was a member of the local VAD, was called from his work at Cowan's and we never saw him for a week. He had been on duty at the infirmary. Some of the soldiers he helped wrote to him for years. I can remember the injured being taken from Carlisle Station on luggage trucks and their moans could be heard all over Court Square.

Tom Lightfoot, December 1968

Wetheral Entertainment

What led me to take up this game was that my father, J.F. Farrer, made the bowling green in his garden (at Wetheral, which was originally a croquet lawn) and I helped him, cutting it and rolling it each day so keeping it in good order for the players. I became the first lady member. Members and their families entertained some of the soldiers who were in hospital in Carlisle after the Gretna railway disaster.

Mrs F.M. Irving, December 1961

Picture House Treats

Groups of wounded soldiers were often entertained to the pictures and their tea in the café. These Picture Houses and cafés were super entertainment for all ages.

M. Hill

Munitions Workers

Seeing these females in their snappy costumes was then a revelation, yet it proved the forerunner of present day outfits. A close-fitting cap to contain the hair, neat tunic with a belt and to complete the effect they wore trousers with a neat crease…The danger these girls lived with every hour, yet they were always in happy spirits. If the atmosphere was humid, the effect [of the chemical vapour] on some of the girls was remarkable, for in a drunken way that savoured of alcohol, they would start to sing or cry and have

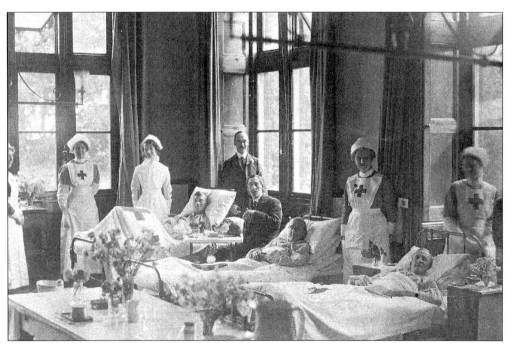

Inside Chadwick Auxilary Hospital in July 1915. The casualties here might be from the Gretna railway disaster.

A group of munition workers photographed in Carlisle. Their 'snappy' costumes are just as Harry Slight described them.

fits of uproarious laughter. Then they were taken to a rest-room to recover. In an explosion…in a press-house on the range, a girl called Black was killed instantly, her partner, Belle McPherson, lost an arm.

Harold Slight, 1962

Bramwell Evens

Many Carlisle people will remember the Revd Bramwell Evens, who came to the city about the outbreak of the 1914-18 war. His Picture House Services in the Botcheregate Picture House, though criticized by some more conservative churchmen met the needs of thousands of munition workers whose only alternative was to walk the streets or pack into the already overcrowded pubs. The Central Hall in Fisher Street is a memorial to his stay in the town. He later made a nationwide name for himself as 'Romany' of the BBC *Children's Hour* and his sudden death left a gap in the program which has never been filled.

Tom Lightfoot, March 1957

Service Pay

I was serving in the Border Regiment in the hottest part of the line at Ypres in Belgium…After two and a half years in the line I was badly disabled in the Battle of the Somme…Fate ordained that I was to find employment at Gretna, early 1917, as a timekeeper, a position I was to hold until the factory's termination. The wages were a Godsend after the service pay of a tanner a day.

Harold Slight, 1962

Women Footballers

Us kids that lived around the neighbourhood…formed a team [in 1917]. My position was right full-back. The opposing team were all women [munition workers], I suppose they were all girls, but they looked like women to a kid of fifteen. The right full-back on the opposing team had the ball and dribbled down the field and passed the ball to me. She found out that she had made a mistake and came after the ball, but got me instead. I will never forget the kick on the shins with those steel toes in the boot.

C. Armstrong

Army Driver

I spent 4 ½ years driving a 6 ton Altion lorry, solid tyres, chain driven and a painted Union Jack on it. At Gretna and Mossband I carried high explosives and towed searchlights and anti-aircraft guns to sites all round the coast. I remember that when we took a gun to Glasson we had to move the gatepost on the gate on Burgh Marsh to get the gun through, but as we had thirty sappers on board they soon made

The East Cumberland Women Munition Workers football team, in Carlisle in 1917. It was probably one of these girls who kicked young Armstrong on the shins.

73

short work of that difficulty. I remember towing a gun to Powfoot for night practice shooting at kites.

William Scott, 1964

Wounded

On 6 April 1917 the Canadians captured Vimy Ridge in France. I was there. The year before 150,000 French soldiers perished trying to take that ridge. Our General was from Victoria BC, a fine wise man. The battle started at daylight and by night the snow was falling and our field guns were on top of the ridge. The Germans retreated 3 miles. I am told that the German reserves were too far back to be of any help. After the terrible ordeal at Passcendaele in Belgium in November 1917, I landed in hospital in Carlisle… in a schoolroom – blackboards and children looking in the windows – not far from a movie theatre. I do not know the name. Then we were moved to another school on Newtown Road…a new building. Miss Lightfoot was my nurse and very nice to me. A wee girls' dancing class put on the Scarf dance for us. A very nice young lady brought me a pie. A lady took a few of us to see *Black Beauty* movie show – it was a wonderful picture. A VAD nurse asked a few of us to her home for dinner one evening. An old lady gave me a bag of 'rusty' apples. How can I forget the kind people of Carlisle?

Thomas Forbes Baxter, April 1976

Conscription

Lakeland had pretty rough road surfaces in the middle of the Great War. No other traffic was visible which is hardly surprising inasmuch as petrol for joy riding was virtually non-existent in 1916. How my uncle wangled it I have no idea. Our own car was laid up for lack of it. Nor do I know how he, an able-bodied and robustly healthy man of great strength and size, managed to avoid conscription, which (if I remember rightly) came in on 2 March 1916

Brian Fawcett, January 1974

No Medal

I was a Border [Regiment] man all my life. When I reached the age of sixteen I joined the Volunteers 1st Batt. Border Regt…I served in 1914-18 with the 1st/4th Battalion through Burma and India. Invalided home in 1919 through malaria. Graded C3 for three years 1916, '17 and '18 and was astounded when discharged at Manchester A1. No disability pension. No Victory Medal.

George (Danny) Doyle, 1958

In The Trenches

After a month in the trenches of Ypres we [the Border Regiment] were coming out for a rest in La Cleet Wood. The time was after midnight and dark. We could vaguely see what appeared to be a kilted regiment on its way to replace another unit. Suddenly

Wounded soldiers and their nurses outside the infirmary wing of the Fusehill Workhouse in 1918 – it was then in use as a military hospital.

a voice hailed form the darkness, 'Is there anyone from Carlisle among you?' I replied 'Yes – Sergeant Harry Slight'. He said 'You remember me – Sergeant McMeekin of the City Police'. I had been in France since 1914 [and was sent the local paper] so when I read of his death in the *Cumberland News*…it struck me forcibly what a fine figure of a man he was in life.

Harold Slight, 1962

Royal Naval Air Service

We were given the full Royal Navy training course; hammock lashing, rope splicing, make and mend and boxing the compass. Very soon after the amalgamation of the RFC and RNAS [to form the RAF in 1918], a Guards regiment, senior NCO came to give us the Army drill; complete with the Army military salute in place of the friendly Royal Navy salute. The navy blue uniform was replaced by khaki, our shoes by boots. Our 'number ones' blue was still allowed for walking out.

A.E. Jolly, ex Sgt. Fitter RAF, March 1969

Peace

My period as a cathedral chorister was 1916 to 1922. In those days we rehearsed in the West Walls choir schoolrooms each day from 9 a.m. to 9.50, then we marched across the abbey to the cathedral for Matins (sung) at

Peace celebrations in Lindisfarne Street on 19 July 1919. There were similar scenes on nearly every street in the city. The effigy is that of the Kaiser, ready to be burnt on a bonfire later in the day.

10 a.m. Afterwards we again crossed the abbey to the playground where for something like 10 minutes or so, we resumed the never-ending soccer match between the boys of Decani and Contoris until lessons commenced at 11 a.m. sharp.

On 11 November 1918 we were engaged in battle when Canon Rawnsley was seen trotting across the abbey towards us. 'Where is your master?' he enquired breathlessly. We answered that Minor-Canon Bark (responsible for our education in the choir school) had not arrived yet. 'Then come with me boys', he cried. We all trotted back with him to the cathedral. Upon arriving, we were taken up the tower, the Union Jack was struck and on the stroke of 11 a.m. we sang *God Save the King*. It was a thrilling experience for throughout the city factory hooters were sounding and the steam from them could be seen rising through the cold November atmosphere.

The Armistice – we were told – had been signed and the war was at an end. Best of all for us, we were given the day off school. We still had to turn up for 4 p.m. evensong of course! There was joy in my home that day for my eldest brother Richard, who had served with the Royal Scots Fusiliers since 1914, was home on leave from the trenches. Great indeed was the rejoicing.

Robert Cecil Routledge, November 1978

CHAPTER 5

Pleasure

Listening to the Band.
Victoria Park, Carlisle.

Evening and Sunday performances in the bandstand at the park were always popular before the First World War.

Program for Algie's Circus, 11 January 1904. By that date his circus was on Collier Lane. It is Algie who is shown as the trainer and in the photograph.

Nero The Lion

The licensee of the Howard Arms was Jack Beatty at that time [1890s] and all the showground people were good customers. Chipperfield's big menagerie visited the Sands for a winter season. They required publicity to get a big audience so they issued a challenge to the public of £50 to anyone who would put their head in a lion's mouth. Jack accepted and the lion selected was Nero, very old and heavily fed beforehand. Beatty was thin and six foot, but a very small head. He knelt down and the attendant opened the lion's mouth. Jack's head was in and out like a flash. He was the city hero for weeks, but on the quiet I think his reward was £5 not £50.

Harold Slight, 1962

Algie's Circus

I am another fan of Algie's Circus for I went every week [and] paid two pence to sit on a wooden form. But it was grand fun…there was all sorts of things at Algies…we were more easily pleased them days than we are today. But it was all good fun and no badness.

Mrs N. McCalla, June 1958

Wet and Wonderful

As I remember Algie's was first [in 1900] where the 'Palace' now stands and moved to Collier Lane when the 'Palace' was to be built. There was always a good show and about three times a year they put on a gigantic 'Water Spectacle'. The ring was covered with waterproof sheets and then filled with huge jets of water illuminated by coloured limelights. Onto the water came boats and steam-boats and a great show was put on with fireworks, men falling in the water and the clowns jumping about. How we kiddies enjoyed the spectacle of the fat policeman in his inflated suit being thrown into the water and floating there on his tummy, too fat to help himself.

Yes Algie's has happy memories for we of the older generation and I for one much preferred the rumbustious entertainment of those days to the synthetic stuff of today.

G.H. Smith, July 1958

Processions

At the age of five I witnessed Queen Victoria's Golden Jubilee [in 1887]. At the age of fifteen I carried a flag in the Diamond Jubilee procession and sang with the combined choirs on the Swifts. Strange to say, I can't remember King Edward's Coronation festivities, but there were many processions such as May Day, before motor cars displaced horses. This brought out a wonderful show of beautiful groomed horses, gay with bright and many coloured ribbons and shining harnesses, drawing splendidly decorated lorries. There were also lifeboat processions, fancy dress cycle parades and to us boys in particular, spell-binding gorgeous circus processions…I could have told you much of Carlisle sixty or seventy years ago, such as when the Border Regiment went off to the Boer War; when itinerant German bands of three or four players, played to the big houses in Chatsworth Square etc., for the entertainment of the residents; when piano-sized organs with picturesque Italian girls went round the streets; when the market was an open one in front of the Town Hall. There you need never be hungry for you could get a tin saucer of green peas and vinegar

Boys follow a circus procession along Castle Street in the 1890s. The circus would be making for the Sauceries where they would pitch tent for a week of performances.

for a ha'penny; where you could see travelling acrobats, musicians and performing bears.

James Beatty, July 1958/September 1965

Dancing Bear

An Italian called Damprosio used to visit the city with a big black dancing bear. In the yard behind Fay's lodging house in Drovers Lane [where he stayed] was a lock-up [where the bear was kept]. On feeding it that morning, although muzzled, it savaged him and the bear broke away. This is what met me on my way up Drovers Lane on my way to Lowther Street School; down the yard ran Damprosio, blood streaming down his face, the bear in pursuit. Finally it was lassoed, assisted by the police. I never saw them again.

Harold Slight, 1962

Fairs

The hirings on the Sands were a real event in those days [1896]. Billy Newsome was the king pin [of the fair] and every year he had something new in entertainment. His elder brother, Charlie Newsome, lived on the Sands all year round and on Saturday used to entertain us kids under the first archway of [the dry] Eden Bridge, with a Punch and Judy puppet show. Generally the Sands square was used by swag jewellery auctioneers, flim-flam artists and escape artists who passed themselves off as ex-sailors. They would have a long rope and they would ask anyone in the crowd

to tie them up in anyway they liked and he would free himself, which they always did, and then he would pass the hat around and anywhere from sixpence to two shillings would be his reward.

Richard Carruthers, March 1959

Pierrots

I was born in Carlisle and lived there for the first twenty years of my life. We went to Silloth for a fortnight's holiday every year, though we also had, some years, an extra one on the Scottish side of the Solway and the east coast. But my father said there was nowhere as good as the Solway. We used to stay with the harbour master, near the blacksmith's shop. Almost every evening we went to the Pierrots. After the war in 1920, we were at Silloth and David Fuller was going strong. I think it is rather a pity there are no entertainments like that now.

Mrs Maud Brotherton, July 1978

Seaside Entertainment

It was soon after the Boer War in 1900 or 1901, when I was fourteen or fifteen years old, that one summer evening we saw two figures in white Pierrot costumes pushing a small piano on a trolley across the Green. They parked the piano behind a small shrubbery facing the steep bank which formed a natural gallery, on the spot which was to be their stand for many years after. We and a few others who had gathered there, sat and listened to the first performance of the Silloth

Pierrots on their favourite pitch at Silloth. Pierrots were a popular attraction for those on holiday at the seaside.

Pierrots. Later in the evening they were joined by a third member who had come off the evening train and those three, David Fuller, George Worthington and Arthur Court, were the original Silloth Pierrots. Fuller, of course, had a fine baritone voice, Worthington was a good musician and pianist and Arthur Court provided the humour in the program. There were mercifully, no pop groups or pop stars in those days, nor were there loud speakers or microphones; yet the singers could make their voices carry without difficulty.

W.J.R. Brown, June 1967

A Canoe Trip

The following relates to my brother Wilson and I and goes back to 1934 or '35, Good Friday. A fine day presented the opportunity for a couple of complete novices to assemble a folding canoe and set off from the [Canal] Sheds, Newtown, for the open sea. An hour or two later we were trying to follow the flow of the river around a maze of sand banks. We could see no land and must have been midway between the two shores when we were startled by the sound of rushing water. In the distance we saw, filling the horizon, a low bank of water bearing down on us. We pointed the craft head on and waited. We were struck by the tidal wave, lifted up and spun round several times in churning white-topped waves. We struggled to keep the canoe upright and only just succeeded. After a while the water calmed down and looking around we noticed that all signs of sand banks had gone and both shores were visible.

As the northern shore was nearer we made for it and eventually got our kit onto a bus at Eastriggs. It was an experience neither of us will forget – it scared us stiff.

Ronald Beattie, November 1961

HM Theatre

I well remember the old plays shown at the 'Vic', as Her Majesty's Theatre was called [in 1895]. The theatre always had a splendid orchestra led by Felix Burns and later by his son, named after his father. The gallery was 3d, pit 6d, orchestra stalls 1s 3d, dress circle 2s 6d and early doors 3d extra.

Richard Carruthers, March 1959

The Fire

I remember well the old 'Vic' [the Victoria Hall, renamed HM Theatre] burnt out in Lowther Street [on 15 September 1904]. Joe Gibson our next door neighbour being in the fire brigade had me sprinting up the Viaduct in the early morning of that day. We were on hand early, aged then, if I remember, fourteen or fifteen. [He was actually seventeen.]

George (Danny) Doyle, 1958

The Matchbox

My father, John Whitfield, who is now nearing his ninety-third birthday, says 'the Matchbox' was a small square building made entirely of wood with a covering of felting and it

The result of the fire at Her Majesty's Theatre on 15 September 1904. The interior was completely gutted and had to be rebuilt.

Her Majesty's Theatre Orchestra, photographed behind the theatre in the 1920s.

was situated on the Sands close to the Turf Hotel. Because of the danger of fire in such a building, my father was forbidden as a boy to go into it, but, nevertheless, he did on more than one occasion pay it a visit and he remembers the late Sims Reeves sing there. It was run as a Variety Theatre and my father says that the management brought really good artistes, both in the world of music and entertainment. He was very young at the time and does not think the theatre lasted very long as it was considered unsafe.

Mrs H. Brown, February 1958

Music Halls

I can remember going to the Matchbox on the Sands to a Salvation Army meeting that was held there. That would be over sixty years ago. The theatre in Rickergate…was situated behind the Scotch Arms, my father-in-law took me to have a look around it about fifty years ago. There was nothing held at that time, but later it was a dance hall. An entrance was made in Peter Street and a staircase led up to the hall. The Ribble bus [garage] is now on the site.

Mr A. Baxter, March 1958

The Star

As a native of Carlisle…a place that is well established in my memory is the Star Music Hall. The front entrance was in Peter Street, but a wide lane ran down the side of the building and led to

A cartoon by Ashton Ridley (a newsagent), of the cinema proprietor, Leon Gould, who owned the Stanley Hall and Star Cinema. Miss E. Ridley wrote in 1973: 'It has been nice to see some of my brother's cartoons. I remember him doing them.'

the gallery entrance, past the back door and side door of the Scotch Arms Hotel and into Rickergate. Mr Henry Stennet, a 'song and dance' artiste, managed the hall for quite a while. Then it went over to boxing and was occupied by the Salvation Army, following [their vacation] of the Matchbox on the Sands and pending the building of their new citadel.

Mr Denis McCauley was the landlord of the Scotch Arns and from there his daughter was married to Seth Chandley, a jockey well established on Northern racecourses.

Peter Clarke, September 1958

The Flics

If I remember rightly the only picture house at that time [1906-1910] was the Public Hall, at which Sydney Bacon proudly presented his 'animated pictures'. A children's matinee was held every Saturday afternoon, the price of admission being one penny. Crowds of us youngsters used to assemble long before opening time and were marshalled into ranks by commissionaires of the ex-NCO type. The films were generally of the cowboy and Indian type, or else stories of the American Civil War, with dashing cavalry charges. The shouts of excitement from the kids drowned the music provided by the piano player, who took advantage of the din to take a short rest from his labours. As each child usually had an apple or an orange, or some other eatable to consume, I have often wondered what a job the cleaning staff must have had to get the place ready for the evening performance.

On occasions the management ran a 'Go as you Please' competition at the evening performance, at which local aspirants to stage fame tried out their apprentice hand. The judging was by the amount of applause, and it was not unknown for friends of a candidate to have a heavy weight tied to a piece of string. The said weight being dropped continuously on the floor contributed in no small measure to the volume of sound. If the efforts of the budding Carusoe, or Robey did not meet with the approval of the audience, he or she was the recipient of 'fruit', both vocal and literal. I understand that on more than one occasion the curtain had to be lowered whilst a stage hand applied bucket and broom [to what]…resembled a garbage heap.

Later Mr Leon Gould opened the Stanley Hall in Botchergate. He offered prizes for regular attendance on Saturday afternoons, and the young patrons were issued with an attendance card similar to those used in Sunday schools. Though a few were attracted by the 'glittering prizes', the majority remained loyal to the Public Hall.

Tom Lightfoot, August 1956

Pooles Myriorama

I actually saw a show…at the New Public Hall, Chapel Street, it being called 'Pooles Myriorama'. This must have been a special program for schools, as our tickets were obtained from the school. Unfortunately I was so young (about seven) my recollections are very vague, but I do remember the painted canvas screens moving on large rollers showing pictorial views of the scenery and events. The scenes were historical and the pictures concerned the Roman Empire.

When we were children we were very keen on magic lanterns and visited one another's houses, where we put

Half-price ticket for Poole's Myriorama at the Public Hall. One of the children attending kept the ticket and later sent it to Mary Burgess.

up a white backboard and in the dark displayed our slides which were made up of small coloured pictures and the illumination in the lantern was from one-candle power!

Wilf Welsh, January 1975

The Public Hall

Respecting the old Catholic church [on Chapel Street]…the building has been of course used for many purposes in latter years. I wonder if anyone remembers Arthur Brigden's Swiss Choir which usually rented what was then known as the New Public Hall, for some three weeks. Or Poole's Myriorama which came to this hall once a year. This show took one round Europe with screens of pictures and a commentary. Tickets were distributed in schools and admission for children to early evenings and Saturdays was one penny plus the 'coupon' ticket. It made a very good geography lesson.

Fred Parker, January 1970

Posters

In the upper parts of most small shop doors, cinema posters were usually displayed behind the glass panes. It could be seen at a glance what was showing at the Public Hall, Stanley Hall, Star Cinema (Rex) or indeed HM Theatre's bill for the week.

D. Laing, May 1976

Cinema Cafés

Mr Sydney Bacon had the first Picture House in Carlisle [in 1906]. The [later] Picture Houses also provided two cafés for Carlisle. The Botchergate Picture House Café with Miss Shields as manageress and the City Picture House Café in English Street with Miss Shaw as manageress. Both were of high standard and very popular cafés. The City Picture House Café was noted for the veranda with its glass top tables. Also for black and white coffees topped with whipped cream.

M. Hill

Curling

The Derwentwater Curling Club, of which I have been president for many years, used to play matches each year – home and away – with Carlisle. We played on a pond at Stanwix somewhere near Sir James Watt's Nursery Gardens and I remember a Carlisle team of Colonel Wm Donald, Wm Carrick and Wm Pratchitt.

Sir Percy Hope, February 1956

Early Train

I may be able to add a small amount of information about the Curling Club…members…Mr W. Donald, later Col…and Mr Todd and my father… the date the winter of 1895. I was just near my teens and had more interest in the skating which took place on part of the pond, but remember the stir of the

Curling on the brickworks pond at Kingmoor, probably during the severe winter of 1895. This is where the Gosling Bridge Hotel is today.

mornings when the team were catching an early train to Lochmaben.

Mrs H. Stewart, February 1956

The Bandstand

As I am the son of the late bandmaster, T. Hills, I can well remember the first band concert given by the Artillery Volunteer Band [in the bandstand in 1894] under the conductorship of my father. I was just seven years of age. I was the boy that gave out the music to the bandsmen. At that age I was just learning to play but not quite good enough to play in the band. Later I played euphonium in St Stephens and Fodens Bands.

James B. Hills, February 1957

Bands

I was very interested…in the old bandstand in the park and very sorry to hear it is coming down. Many an enjoyable night I have spent listening to the bands; my own father (Felix Burns) conducted the Border Regiment Band and listening to *The Merry Widow* and *Merry Wives of Windsor* sounded okay. But those were the days when music was music. The park won't look the same without it, even the seats around it were so comfortable, but these things happen and time marches on.

Mrs Winifred Strong, February 1957

Roller Skating Rink

The enterprise commenced in a lavish manner [in 1909] with orchestra, four instructors and a lady instructor, but its prosperity was short-lived. The novelty soon disappeared. I remember the holding of a carnival at which my cousin, Hilda Hilton won ladies first prize. The place was so packed little skating was possible.

Regarding the skating rink fire, I saw this standing near Petteril Bridge on Warwick Road. The flames were so bright I imagined it was the grandstand at Brunton Park...I ran to the scene of the fire in time to see the front collapse in one piece.

P. Wardle, May 1957

Indoor Skating

My memory goes back to the winter of 1914-15, when stationed with the 'Lonsdales' at Blackwell Racecourse. Many more of the surviving members of this battalion, will no doubt remember the skating rink, at which we sometimes spent our evenings. The main floor was reserved for experienced skaters and some not so experienced. At one side were small penned off enclosures for learners, which were a source of great amusement to watchers.

Frank Graves, May 1957

Rink's Use

Teenagers of today may find it difficult to believe that Carlisle once possessed a full-sized skating rink...Its occupation during [the First World War as a munition works] and then, later on, the rink was once used by Morton Sundour Fabrics Ltd for the purpose of the examination of a huge hand-tufted carpet, as they had no space

in their darning department, at that time...before the disastrous fire of 1920.

Oscar Unrah, June 1957

Listening In

At home we had one of the latest radio sets and this was powered by a 120 volt high tension battery; a wet battery, or as they were known, an accumulator. The latter had to be recharged and topped up with distilled water at regular intervals and had to be taken to Carrudice's, where they loaned you another one for a fee of sixpence, until your own was ready. The batteries soon ran down, however, and to hear a broadcast then the ear had to be held near the loudspeaker.

D. Laing, May 1976

Football

At Brunton Park...in late 1908 and early 1909, the ground was being laid out as a football field and the Corporation dustmen were allowed to tip their ashes etc. round the pitch to form a banking. After school hours a number of my classmates and myself used to go to Brunton Park to see if there were any useful articles (to boys) in the rubbish heap and we got quite a lot from time to time.

I remember the last match on Devonshire Park against Accrington Stanley on 29 April 1909. It happened to be my birthday and as a special treat my father took me to the match and that was the first time I had been in the

LISTENING IN
IT'S NOT ALL PLEASURE

A comic radio postcard with the postmark dated 1925. This is of the period that D. Laing was listening to the radio in Barwise Nook.

grandstand. I also recall the 'friendly' against Newcastle United, because on that day [24 September 1908] Princess Louise was visiting the city (not to see the match of course).

Jimmy Bell, October 1969

Early Players

I saw my first vision of a football match on Borough Grounds at the age of three...I can still name the majority of the players like Herb Ivinson (newsagent in Denton Street), England in goal; the St Pat schoolmaster, Capt Frank Ross, and Hawthorn Brown to name a few. Those were football days. The top players, about 1895, were then paid £3 a week, a whale of a wage when a top class journeyman was 25s a week

and glad of, after serving your time for seven years at 2s 6d to 3s a week.

George (Danny) Doyle, 1958

Dour Fans

When I was six, our family moved from Scotland to Carlisle in late 1919 or early 1920. Our house was in the middle of a long terrace in Warwick Road, the road which runs east from the city centre to Brunton Park, the home ground of Carlisle United. When I grew older, I was to learn with interest that our house had been the birthplace of the mother of President Woodrow-Wilson (her father was a Congregationalist minister in the city), but what interested me as a small boy was the view it gave me of the Saturday afternoon football crowd. At

Carlisle United in front of the grandstand on Devonshire Park, sometime between 1904 and 1909. Written on the back of the postcard is the message, 'Owing to the very bad state of Devonshire Park your replay with St Patricks will be on Monday night instead of tonight'.

half-past two a dour, silent procession of middle-aged men in cloth caps and white mufflers would trudge past our front door.

There followed three hours of silence (broken occasionally by a distant roar, if the wind was in the right direction) and then the procession would come trudging back. If their dourness was unchanged, United had won. If they looked even grimmer than before, they had lost…if the match had been of special interest (say a cup-tie), I might pluck up courage to go out and ask one of the gloomy men what the score had been.

Dr Alistair Ross, February 1978

Picnics

On a Co-op employees picnic at Wreay, rain had fallen so we

crowded into the inn. I remember that occasion well. Perhaps I'd be sixteen or seventeen. Anyway, someone had put my name in the hat asking for singers. Even with my experience as a choir boy, I was shy at singing solo. However, I plucked up courage and sang a song my brother had sang, Harry Lauder's *Killiecrankie*, for which I was well applauded. By the way, it wouldn't have been 'the done thing' for a church choir to have a sing-song in an inn.

James Beaty, September 1965

Hammond's Pond

As far as I remember Hammond's Park was officially opened to the public on Whit Monday 1923. I was asked by Mr Hammond if I could provide a concert party for this special event. The song *Pleasureland*, especially written for the occasion by Wm Coulthard of Mayson Street, was sung by Arthur Mingins [comedian] and was greatly appreciated by the huge audience who joined in singing the chorus heartily. After the concert the second boating pond was opened and as it was a fine day the crowds enjoyed themselves.

Mr Tinning, June 1973

Former Brickworks

Archie Hammond was my uncle and I knew the place long before it was opened to the public. Certainly the lake at the Blackwell Road end was formed as the result of excavating for brick-making purposes nearby, but [I] am uncertain as to how the rest of the lake came into being. I know what a job it was to keep it fairly clear of weed. The usual procedure was for one person to row the boat and another to trail a scythe through the water to cut the weed which was very prolific in the early days and often spoilt the rowing.

My uncle had great ideas for Pleasureland and it was unfortunate that the lack of finance prevented his carrying out a lot of them. The older generation will remember the original open-air dance floor and the attempt to start a small 'zoo'. I recall one of the monkeys escaping for several days and running mischievous riot in Upperby before being cornered.

Arthur J. Lacey, June 1973

Escaped Monkey

I lived in Henderson Road. My daughter Agnes Law, was in the

Another of the attractions at Hammond's Pond was the open-air model railway circuit. There are more men than boys showing interest as this LNWR model runs past.

scullery when in popped the monkey. Thinking it was a dog she stroked it. Then it jumped onto the piano, from there to the kitchen dresser and started throwing cups off the shelf, finally [it] hurled a cream jug. Jumping again on to the table it then made outside for Constable Biggar's baby's pram.

By that time, Robert Morrow of Scalegate Road made an effort to catch it…it bit his thumb having been caught. It was quite an exciting day for everyone. My daughter, now living in Coventry, recalls the day she stroked the monkey. Mr Hammond gratefully repaid me for the damage it had done.

Mrs M.J. Ashton, August 1962

The Last Prize Fight

On the outskirts of this city, a field which is now the site of the electricity station, down Willow Holme, was where the last prize fight took place. Although just a youth at the time of this event, I was a spectator by chance one Sunday morning. The conditions that made it a Prize Fight (although illegal) were strictly observed by both combatants, stripped to the waist, belt and trousers only and bare fists.

This fight was between Willie Turnbull and Jimmy Swailes, both of Caldewgate. Now this was the result of Swailes baiting Turnbull on a Saturday night in a public house of that area. Turnbull a young but strong youth was enjoying a drink with his friend when in came Swailes who was much taller and older. He eventually went too far with his insults, so it was agreed to meet and fight to a finish.

It was on that very morning that I was on the Sheepmount, which was then a huge city ash tip and it was a familiar sight to see men with dogs or ferrets killing the numerous rats there. On looking under the railway bridge we saw a crowd from Willow Holme making towards the canal side [he means 'The Cut', a millrace]. We were told of the fight so joined in with the crowd. As the fight started there could have been 800 persons present, even the mother of Swailes was there to cheer him on.

After a time Swailes with his long flailing arms seemed to be in the lead, but Turnbull was tough and hit hard to the stomach…then came a dramatic interruption from the policeman on that beat. He had come quietly up behind and shouted to the fighters to stop. He was immediately ringed by tough dealers or 'diddles' as we called them and told to watch it like them. They kept a look-out on his whistle. Turnbull was getting the upper hand now with his heavy hitting and there was blood on Swailes face. Suddenly there was the sound of police whistles and the crowd ran everywhere. With the policeman being overdue from his beat and knowing this locality for trouble, they came in the 'Black Maria' van from Devonshire Walk and Willow Holme.

The two combatants and also spectators were arrested but I fared better for being small. I made a fast getaway to hide among the bushes in the Caldew, sitting in the water. The *News of the World*, which had the largest circulation at that time, came out with the glaring headlines: 'The World's Last Prize Fight Takes Place In Carlisle'.

Harold Slight, 1962

CHAPTER 6

Consumers and shopkeepers

This must have been the smallest shop in Carlisle, a butcher's on Greystone Road.

Market Day

I was born in 1903, my mother [being the] daughter of a village blacksmith. My grandparents farmed at Rockliffe Cross and attended Carlisle Market each Saturday. They drove a very smart pony and high gig which was climbed into by two iron steps at the side and had a large umbrella to cover them both when raining.

When dressed for market grandmother wore a small bonnet, which to me seemed perched on top of her head and tied with broad ribbons under her chin, black dress of silky material and cape which went over her shoulders. Grandfather wore a hard hat which was tall and square, starched collar and cravat. He was clean shaven but had bushy side whiskers, longish coat, cut away at the front and 'tails' at the back.

He was a non-smoker but used snuff.

I can remember going to Carlisle with them in the gig which was 'put up' in the mews. I think it was in Peter Street. There was dozens of horses and traps in these mews at that time. Many stalls round the Town Hall…sold everything you could mention. There was a number of stalls too along by the old gaol and at one stall was sold 'Gaol Toffee', which was known by all visiting town. Nearer the station sat 'Blind Tommy' who played an organ or harmonium. He belonged to Causeway Head, Silloth and played the organ in the church there.

Jas Maxwell, 1957

In February 1888 work was progressing on the construction of the Covered Market. Roof members are here being lifted into place.

Market Rooms

I remember some of the lanes between Scotch Street and Lowther Street being lined with traps behind one another, their shafts dropped to the ground all in an orderly fashion – the horses were stabled nearby while the farmers and their wives visited the markets and did their shopping in the city. Rickergate on Saturdays was a hub of activity with conveyances from the country. Each of the many inns had market rooms where baskets were left and also parcels received from the tradesmen for collection by their customers. A woman was on duty to deal with these and take charge.

Wilf Welsh, December 1973

Paddy's Market

When my father was farming at Curthwaite, he used to bring me into Carlisle with potatoes to sell in Paddy's Market on Saturdays, 6d a stone and he gave away any not sold. I remember horse buses coming round the castle corner and changing horses at the Town Hall.

William Scott, 1964

Covered Market

To read about the opening of the 'New Market'…recalled memories of my childhood. I was taken by my parents to see the illuminations which marked the occasion [in 1889]. I well remember the gas star near the clock,

another opposite Corrys the butchers, and one near the Fisher Street entrance. All round the Town Hall…and English Street the buildings were outlined by 'fairy lights' (little glass bottles or jars which I presume would contain night lights). Torches were carried by some people and there was a firework display. The din and the intensity of the crowd frightened me.

My parents carried me through St Cuthberts Lane to West Walls where we stopped and watched the glare and heard the subdued noise of the fireworks from Fawcett's School door. When the excitement had died down my parents took me to bed at grandma's (the Plough Inn, Caldewgate). I was born in Stanwix in 1883.

T.M. Forster, September 1963

Shopping

When I went shopping with my mother on Saturday nights, either in Liptons or the old Maypole, I was fascinated how these fellows patted a pound of butter into those squares just like a building brick. That always interested me, but there is no more of that stuff.

C. Armstrong

Ready-made Trousers

I never thought the day would come when women would be able to go into a store to buy ready-made trousers for themselves.

Florence Wheeler, 1969

The Maypole on the Viaduct corner is where Mr C. Armstrong went shopping with his mother.

Was James Robinson's shop the oldest such establishment in the city? It was known as the Eagle Stores when seen here in Shaddongate.

Sweets

To a young lad there was plenty to look at in the shop windows of busy Caldewgate…one day I looked in the window of Adam Nichol (groceries merchant). In the window were several small dishes containing biscuits of different shapes and sizes, and being in the possession of a penny, I went into the shop and asked for a penny worth… only to be told that I couldn't have those, because they were dog biscuits! It didn't matter because further along Downies sweet shop had aniseed balls 20 a penny, Bobby Dazzlers 12 a penny and plenty more like gob stoppers 2 a penny.

D. Laing, May 1976

Eagle Stores

One business begun by my late husband's grandfather in 1860, was James Robinson & Son…this began in Botchergate, then moved to James Street, thence to Shaddongate, where it was well known as the Eagle Stores and eventually to 93 Lowther Street. The system, begun nearly 100 years ago of travelling round villages and farms taking orders for feeding stuffs as well as groceries, is still in operation although of course, the use of horse-drawn wagons was long since abandoned and many of our customers live in town, not in the country. After the original James Robinson's death, his son, also named James, ran the business and was succeeded on his death in 1936 by his son Arthur. He took Mr Johnston into partnership in 1940 so that he could go into the RAF.

The late Harry Banks was also a partner for a few years before his retirement. After my husband's return from war service, a limited company was formed in 1946 and it was just two years later that he died…Mr Johnston very ably carries on.

Constance Robinson, February 1957

Ridley's Newsagent

My brother Ashton Ridley, had his first newsagent and tobacconist's shop under the old Port Road Bridge, which had to come down [for widening in 1914]. We lived then in Canal House, which I believe at one time was the Custom House when the old canal was there.

Miss E. Ridley, November 1973

Advertising

There is one little piece of advertising that always caught my eye: 'When its eyesight bother consult Mr Strother', on Citadel Row. A few of the shops that were there in my time were F.W. Tassell & Son, the Northampton Boot Co., Bullough & Co., Carlisle Rubber Co., Studholmes, Fred Robson's, James Brown of Lowther Street, Lomas Fishmongers, Clark Bros of Scotch Street, Joe Dent, Fitzsimmons Hats and my old favourite Campbell Browns. I am still wearing one of their trilby hats. I have quite a few memories of my old home town.

C. Armstrong

Cooper's on English Street was another of many grocery shops in the city centre.

The Club

With a growing family [in the 1920s] mother had, like everybody else, to budget carefully. So it was that she joined a 'Universal Club', run by a neighbour. This was a mail-order club and there was nothing that cost more than £1. The secretary would obtain 19 people who wished to purchase something from his catalogue and who was willing to pay a shilling a week. The money collected would be sent off each week and the goods required by a particular member would be sent. This would go on for nineteen weeks then the secretary got the 20th week free for running the club. This was his payment.

Mother got a wall clock with chimes, a pair of bronze statuettes, two dining chairs, a portable gramophone and records, all for £1 a time over the years.

D. Laing, May 1976

Treats

As a child I lived with my parents, sisters and brothers (eleven in all) on Solway Terrace, Corporation Road, so was quite familiar with Rickergate. We were very poor, my father being a painter and decorator; in those days no pensions or relief. So the only means of us children getting cash was running errands or taking people's babies out. We had no more than 1d per week, which had to go a long way. We attended St Marys church and Sunday school and we used to save a ½d to give to collections for black children. So on the way via Rickergate we used to call in Ben Rolley's, next door to Hannah Baty's and get ½d of toffee or sweets. Then opposite was Miss Kirkbride who sold sweets on Sundays. Near was Mary Ann Smiths. I can see her yet leaning over her half door with such rosy cheeks just like her red apples in the shop window. When we were in clover, we would go and spend a 1d and sit down in the back of the shop to a 1d meat pie with lots of gravy. Didn't they taste good. Then my mother dealt at the Co-op which was near and I used to go for flour, a stone twice weekly. Higher up was the tripe shop where we used to get ¼lb for father's tea once weekly.

Ella Middleton (née Kennedy), March 1959

Carlins

Carlin Sunday…is two Sundays before Pasche egg day (Easter Sunday). These carlins were served to customers in the inns and I've heard of competitions. The winner had to eat the most number of platefuls. The prize an ounce of 'bacca' and a clay pipe.

Jas Maxwell, 1957

A Varied Choice

In the far distant days every sitting at the table was a meal to be enjoyed and the choices were varied! Broth, lentil soup, liver, tripe, pigs ear, tail or feet or cows heels, provided by people like Ann Walters on Paddy's Market.

Smoking

Cigarettes, Woodbines, 1d a packet of five and five matches. Remember the song *5 little fags in a dainty little packet* sung by Florie Ford. Capstain cigs 6d a packet of ten. Tobacco 3d an ounce. You could get as many cuttings (end pieces) to last a week for a penny, when tobacco was tobacco…not filtered up with saltpetre to make it burn faster and eat your guts out. One noggin of whisky 6d and you knew you had had it. Gill of ale 1d – take a jug and it was filled no matter what size.

Hundreds of times of Friday nights have I ran from Denton Holme to the Sally Port with a jug for hot tripe and onions, or a delicious dish called 'sheep bags', a quart jug full for 2d. Those were the days.

George (Danny) Doyle, 1958

Tattie Pies

Some old Carlisle folk would give something today for a Caddell's tattie pie in the market.

T. Hetherington, December 1958

Dripping

The Crown & Mitre Inn and Coffee House was partly on both English Street and Castle Street. It covered an extensive site and the kitchens were entered from St Cuthbert's Lane. Here workmen are preparing it for demolition in 1902.

The Railway Tavern can be seen in this 1897 view of the top end of Botchergate. Parker's ironmongers is on the right.

I remembers about the coffee house in my day sixty years ago…a lot of us young girls knew what day to go to the coffee house. It was up St Cuthberts Lane to the back. We got 3d off our mothers and a good big basin and we went and got threepenny worth of the best dripping you ever tasted. Butter was cheap but it [dripping] was cheaper and we loved it. I had carlins, they were grand too. We got them from the Bug and Flea and do you know where that was? Just where Jenkin's Brothers shop is today in Fisher Street. You see there was not a lot of money those days…we were all poor but happy…we are not half as happy today.

Mrs N. McCalla, March 1962

Coffee House Kitchen

I too can remember often going into the kitchen of the old coffee house and seeing large joints swinging from the bottle-jack.

Miss A. Dawson, August 1960

Rope and Twine

101

As a native of Carlisle – born 19 June 1877 in Randleston Lane, Botchergate, or Todd's Court as it was more often called – I am very much interested [in the city]. The late Joe Nixon was rope spinning on a piece of ground behind the old Railway Tavern – between Saddle Lane and the back of Portland Place. It was also a quoit alley and running track [when] the Watsons [had] the tavern. I turned the big wheel for Joe…all his work during the week being bought by farmers on Saturday after market. His sister was my wife's mother. If there was anything he liked better than a glass of Nelson's Blood – as he called it – rum to be precise, it was two. He was a character and a bonny singer. I would like to give you some facts…but am afraid my writing days are over.

William Johnston, 1957

Railway Tavern

The Railway Tavern was formerly the Saddle Inn, probably after moving from Fisher Street, then it became the Golden Quiot. The tavern would close in 1916.

When the 'State Control Board' took over they stopped the sale of alcohol by chemists and grocers. Today we are back to square one and supermarkets are enjoying the boom. The site of the Railway Tavern now houses Templeton's [supermarket] which will possibly sell more spirits and canned beers in one night than three inns sold in their entire existence.

Simon Keiling, December 1972

Lystor's Ropeworks

Carlisle Square is now getting pulled down in Blackfriars Street opposite Brucciani's shop. My father and grandfather had a factory and shop down there, rope and twine. They lived at 'The Park', Scotby.

F.W. Lystor, November 1963

Saddle Lane

I well remember when I was a very small girl going week by week to the butcher's shop, Mr and Mrs Marks in Portland Place. We used to call at the grocer's shop too, on the corner of Portland Place and Botchergate. I think the next shop to this one was an ironmongers. There was a public house next to Saddle Lane – there was a number of cottages in this lane and a piece of square ground which my father had as a rope and twine business [before 1897], where he spun ropes from a spinning wheel which was turned by a young man. I found a billhead a few weeks ago 'Joseph Nixon, Rope and Twine Spinner', I've been told my father was called 'Gentleman Joe'.

Next to Saddle Lane, Mr Wannop had a grocers business, then a drapers along this part and a confectioners, both I think, belonged to the Bells and were near to Mary Street.

Mrs A.B. Lamonby, November 1957

Mark's the butchers on Portland Place – just as Mrs Lamonby would have remembered it.

Sawyer the Chemist

Henry Sawyer the chemist, I remember very well as I was a customer of his. He made a very good cough mixture and during the winter months I went for the family supply to his shop. The week before he was going to Australia I called for a bottle. He was in great spirits and told me that he had not a decent holiday for fifty or sixty years, mostly behind his counter, but he was going to Australia and have the time of his life having a holiday with his son. He showed me his sun helmet (he had under the counter, with several things to wear in the hot climate). He put the helmet on several times…I wished him the 'best of luck' and a good time with his son. One day I read that Henry had passed away on board ship on his way, before he met his son, and was buried at Aden. It would be a shock for his son.

Miss M.A. Armstrong, November 1960

Henry Sawyer advertises his own 'tic' powder for toothache. The postmark date on this card is 1905.

Far From Home

It was during my off-duty hours as a telephone operator at the Aden General Telephone Exchange (during my services with the RAF in 1936) that I visited the British Cemetery where I came across the grave: Henry Sawyer, died 28 August 1926 in his 75th year. As a native of Carlisle, I remember during my youth the chemist's shop, but since leaving Carlisle in 1930 to join the RAF, I have been but a visitor to my home town.

Patrick McKnespiey, December 1958

Tic Powder

I was born and bred in Carlisle. I remember Henry Sawyer, he used to sell tic powder, a sure cure for toothache. We used to have a box in the house as my parents were great believers in them. I remember a calendar we had, a boy with his face wrapped up advertising tic powders. I hope someone else remembers. I often wish they were still on the market.

Mrs Haughan, 1960

Sure Cures

It may be of interest to know that Sawyers bronchial cough mixture, pastilles and tic powders are still available, even these days of large combines selling cough mixtures and cold and flu powders. We still sell more Sawyers original formula than all the other proprietors put together. Sawyers mixtures has certainly been a good sell over the last 120 years and still seems to be very popular even with the younger generation.

G. Watson Clark (proprietor of Henry Sawyers Chemists), January 1961

Clogs

I was the youngest daughter of John Graham Moffat of Port Road. My father was a painter and decorator along with my fine brothers. My dad was Scotch born in Dumfries and my mother was Agnes Keddy and she came from Wigton. I married Charles McSkimming and he's a Carlisle chap too.

I came for a visit in 1955 and visited a very dear friend in Shaddongate, John Potter. He had a shoe store. When I was a girl of school age he made all my clogs and as old as the dear old fellow was, he made a pair of clogs to bring back to Canada with [me].

Mrs C. McSkimming, May 1964

Cloggers

J. Carruthers, the clogger, had a little shop near the entrance to Shane's yard [in Bridge Street, Caldewgate]. It was grimly old fashioned and the window was full of clog uppers and various types of clog. The door was usually wide open and there was a worn counter and a wooden form against the wall.

Potential customers requiring new

irons or 'coakers' [caulkers], would enter the shop, sit on the seat and take off their clogs, passing them over to Johnny, who usually sat at his last, surrounded by piles of new bottoms, boxes of nails and accoutrements of his trade. He was always busy and his hammering on the last could be heard before reaching the shop. Clogs were in great demand being a popular form of footwear. They kept the feet warm and dry and were cheap to keep in good repair.

D. Laing, May 1976

Nipits

I laughed when I read about Teasdale's Nipits, because my late father [Frank Thompson, an optician] was never without them and sang their praises to all and sundry, even after he retired to Scarborough.

Mrs G. Maud Petterson, July 1958

Fish and Chips

Speculating who was the first...to offer for sale fried fish and chips... two have continued to give the trade a lifetime of service...Perkins, Portland Place (1895) and Joe McSkimmings, Caldewgate, still going strong after sixty years or more. Prior to the more attractive establishments of today, ordinary cottage property was found convenient to accommodate the weird cooking contraptions, generally stone platforms erected over a coal fire, the side walls retaining the heat, which in turn rose to platform level creating a

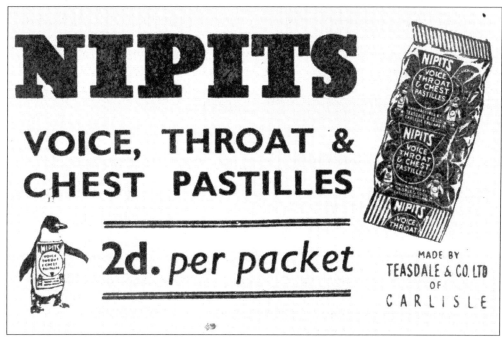

Teasdale's Factory in Denton Holme made all manner of sweets, however only their pastilles had medicinal properties.

practical hot plate. The large circular pans with reinforced bases boiled the fat and the chips, amidst an atmosphere of acrid smoke from the coal fires. In latter years the adoption of wash-house boilers, curtailed a little of the offensive smells.

Simon Keiling, August 1958

Royal Fish

It would be safe to say that not more than half a dozen sturgeon have been caught in the Solway since the beginning of this century. The last to be caught was about 1930 at Loch & Dornock Fisheries when my father was manager. This was offered to His Majesty via the Master of the Household but was refused and permission given for the fish to be sold. Because of the local interest in the unusual catch, the late G.S. McGlasson displayed it on the window slab of his fish shop in St Albans Row, where it remained for two days before being sent to Billingsgate for sale. The proceeds were given to charity.

An interesting sequel was to follow. The catch of this sturgeon interested HM Receiver of Wrecks who tried to lay claim to the fish under the belief that because HM had refused the offer it must then become the property of the Receiver of Wrecks. A great amount of correspondence was involved which went on for many months culminating in the last letter my father wrote… [asking the Receiver] to quote a precedent. We still await a reply.

A.T. McGlasson, May 1975

Off Comers

Rickergate had its characters…as well as a sprinkling of German and Italian traders and before Brucciani's fish and chip period, cheerful Antonio retailed 'pea and tatie' suppers and made ice cream, getting the ice during a hard winter from the Eden and storing in sawdust.

J.J. Proudfoot, November 1960

Drovers

Memories of geese over Eden Bridge are most vivid to me and in my mind's eye I can clearly envisage the many times I saw this interesting sight. The geese were brought into market on foot from the north in great numbers, their movements controlled by several drovers. After they cleared the wider areas around Stanwix they converged on and completely blocked the bridge, bringing to a standstill any vehicular traffic, all horse-drawn [at that time].

Stan Goldsworthy, July 1974

Licensed Traders

Licence arm badges were issued for a fee by the police station then situated on West Walls. Licensing erased brutal drovers such as 'Natey' Davidson, 'Black' Kent and others. Among the better element were Joe McCall, Billy Cant and Wooler. In those days after a sale, it was nothing to the drover to walk to Longtown,

Hethersgill or Brampton and find his own way back.

Others licensed were outside porters and newsboys. The outside porter, after hiring the barrow, could be out all day with a commercial traveller. Newsboys included the casual sellers of Nicholson & Cartner's coloured picture postcards of prominent parts of the city (6 for 2d). With the 1914-18 war it lapsed.

Harold Slight, 1962

Good Pay

When we lived at Longtown a drover named 'Charlie' brought cattle to the farm from Carlisle, perhaps fifty head. He was paid 2s 6d and his supper, which doesn't seem much today, but would be good pay at that time.

Jas Maxwell, 1957

Carlisle Biscuits

William Slater was the son of a Bassenthwaite farmer. He settled early in life at Carlisle and started to make biscuits in premises, long since pulled down, in Scotch Street. These were situated where the entrance to the market is now. After some years the business outgrew this bakery and in 1852 it was transferred to a large factory in James Street. Like so many Victorian manufacturers of food products, William Slater was a Quaker.

F.S. Sanderson, June 1956

CHAPTER 7

Work

The truth behind the stick-men! Women can be seen here in the St Nicholas Firewood Factory tying the chopped sticks into bundles.

Leaving School

When I left school aged thirteen, I started work for 3s a week. A pound a week was the average wage for a labouring man. Skilled labourers were paid around 35s to £2 10s a week. But then butter was 6d a pound, bread was 2d a loaf and ½d 'flam' bought at Carrs was a meal in itself for a growing boy. Coal 1s 8d cwt and coke much cheaper. The buses drawn by horses and owned by Dick Crosby were a penny fare anywhere on the route. A schoolboy would think himself rich with 3d a week pocket money. Here in Canada my grandchildren think I'm kidding when I tell them of my boyhood days in Carlisle. At the age of sixteen here boys think its time their parents bought them a car of their own. We were lucky if we had a bicycle at their age.

Richard Carruthers, June 1959

Poorly Paid

I was born in 1879 so excuse my writing and spelling as I am not so good at it now. When I started work at fourteen, I worked eleven hours a day Sunday to Sunday and every day as a daily maid for 2s 6d a week. What could you get out of that?

Mrs N. McCalla, June 1958

Long Hours

My first job at thirteen, was errand boy at Wilson Jespers (now Border House), English Street. Start work 8 a.m., dust round the shop until any message. An hour for dinner, 12 to 1, with a parcel to deliver in the journey home. Of course we finished work at 8 p.m. up to Friday when there was a lot to do and generally about 9 p.m. when I got home. Saturdays we started as usual, but that was that. Sometimes that day we didn't have much fun because on occasions it was rather late when we reached home, say about 11 p.m....after two or three messages over Stanwix after 8 p.m....sometimes with a parcel you could have shoved in your waistcoat pocket. Sixty-four hours a week at 3s a week.

George (Danny) Doyle, 1958

Getting Hired

I might have gone to farm work. A Wigton farmer offered me £8 board and lodgings for the half year, which was about the wage for a boy of fourteen.

Jas Maxwell, 1957

Apprenticeship

Joe Blain's shop with the 'brush', recalls to me an old story. As an apprentice boy at Sewell's Saddlers, Scotch Street, over sixty years ago, I was sent to Blain's shop for the 'cocoa fibre mats' that were made in the prison. These were special ones made for carriages. They were not ready so I had to take back the following message, 'Tell Mr Sewell from Mr Blain that he will have to wait a bit longer because

Unfortunately the name of this engine driver, seen also on page 13, is unknown. He was nearing retirement at the Canal Sheds, with probably a lifetime on the railways, when this photograph was taken in about 1950.

there are not many prisoners in gaol at present'. Joe Blain was very emphatic that I should take back a correct answer. I had many journeys to Blain's shop but I have never forgotten the one for the carriage mats.

Richard Graham, July 1957

On the Railway

I was employed on the railway for nearly forty-eight years – starting on the LNWR (at 'The Lanky' [Upperby Shed] in 1914, a few months before the outbreak of the Great War) and was on the main line – fireman and driver from 1916, until I retired in 1962…I could tell you some stories of the hectic days and of marvellous little engines we called 'Jumbos', i.e. 2-4-0s, passenger locos. I fired on most of them from time to time, including *Hardwicke*, *Reynard*, *Belted Will*, *Madge*, *Skiddaw* and many others and I never knew one break down.

By the way, I also manned the Royal Scot; the Coronation (on its inception in 1937) and The Caledonian (first driver Carlisle-London on 17 June 1957) and several royal trains, both as fireman and driver and my last turn of duty was the 11.40 p.m., London-Carlisle.

J.F. Stalker, September 1974

Cycling Home

My brother Edwin had a better cycle than mine and this was borrowed occasionally by my father, who was at that time, a fireman on the railway. He was working on the trains to Langholm and on certain weeks worked the shift where the last train to Langholm ended its run there and the engine was put away. The result was, of course, that father had to make his own way home to Carlisle. This he managed by borrowing Edwin's bike, taking it in the guard's van and biking home.

This he did for a period of two years. Occasionally he would break down and then he had to leave the bike

Joe (Nobby) Clark, the sweep, is being helped to bag soot by Anne Leach after cleaning her chimney at 46 Newton Road in the early 1930s.

somewhere for Edwin to collect the following day and walk home or beg a lift. Sometimes finishing earlier he would be in time to catch the last bus to Carlisle.

D. Laing, May 1976

Baking Bread

Looking back, I realise that my mother had a hundred and one jobs. There would be for instance, baking day. We had, as usual then, a fire grate [a range] with an oven. To heat the oven, a damper had to be pulled outwards. This was a knob above the oven, which drew the fire through an aperture underneath the oven, there heating it up. She would set to work mixing the dough and this was put into a large bowl to stand on the 'fender board' in front of the fire, covered by a clean towel and allowed to rise. Then the required quantities were put into bread tins, put into the oven and baked.

The smell of that bread was lovely, but the finished bread even more so. A slice of home-made bread with butter and some jam, was a meal in itself. She made teacakes, apple, rhubarb, currant, custard and jam pies and tarts, shortbread and gingerbread. The taste was out of this world.

D. Laing, May 1976

Washing Day

Another day would be washing day. Up early and down stairs to light the 'copper' fire, under the boiler in the

112

Just another of mother's jobs keeping the house clean. This is an advert in a booklet sent to Mary Burgess by a reader of the *Cumberland News*.

washhouse. The water boiling [soon] the clothes were bubbling over the top and my mother would be 'possing' in a large tub with a 'poss stick', then rubbing them on the rubbing board in a dolly tub and wringing them through a large iron mangle. It was all hard work to wash clothes in those days [1920s]. She usually finished with two or three lines of clothes flapping in the breeze. She also did my grandmother's washing and this was ironed. I had to deliver it to Jane Street in an old pram.

D. Laing, May 1976

Mother's Varnish

My mother varnished the chair and table legs regularly, to keep them tidy, and for this she used a home-made varnish of her own mixture. A note bearing the required ingredients and a fruit-sized bottle had to be taken to Peter Simpson, the chemist. He measured quantities of shellac, Bismark brown and methylated spirits into the bottle. This had to be shaken vigorously and the varnish was ready. She would pour some in an old saucer and apply to all the chair legs where they were scratched.

D. Laing, May 1976

Hetherington & Carruthers

My father, Thomas Carruthers (in partnership with Mr Hetherington) started an oil delivery

Messrs Brown's oil van used to deliver lamp fuel around the country area. Mr Castlehow, the last driver, could even remember the horses – Dick and Polly.

department before I began my apprenticeship about 1886. He planned the fortnightly rounds. The oil was supplied from Liverpool by Bamur [?] & Co. and many a full and empty cask I have trundled up and down Packhorse Lane.

The full casks weighed about 3 ½cwt and were hauled up onto a gantry – I then had to use a brace and 1 ¼ inch bit to bore the hole to insert the tap and from this the 10 gallon drums were filled. We had just one horse and trap and carried about 100 gallons. I can well remember my father's anxiety on foggy and slippery nights when the man was late returning.

J. Arthur Carruthers, November 1959

Lamp Oil

I am the man who can tell you about G.F. Brown and Co.'s shop and van. I was the last man to drive the two horses before they were sold (when the business changed hands). After Mr Brown died, it was bought by Messrs Altham of Penrith and they did not want the oil trade. The stables and van were kept in Barton's Yard where the Lonsdale Cinema now stands. The picture of the van shows Mr Forrester holding the horses heads (Dick and Polly) and was taken in front of Mr Barton's and Dr Fairlie's loose boxes where now stands the GPO. Packhorse Lane was next to the shop on English Street, where the van was backed up and tanks filled with White Rose and

Royal Daylight oil. The fortnightly journeys were originated by my father for Messrs Hetherington & Carruthers and he went round with a new man every year and showed him round the country.

The van was saturated with oil and you won't believe it, it was sold to Mr Rae the confectioner of Brook Street and the coach builders stripped it and had four men with wet swabs ready when the boss set the van on fire. As soon as the oil burnt out and the frame was alight it was put out by swabbers. It took three or four days burning. It was successful and carried bread and cakes for years about and around Carlisle.

J.P. Castlehow, October 1959

Barton's Yard

When I was a boy 25 English Street was the shop occupied by Messrs Hetherington & Carruthers…their stables in Warwick Road, was generally called Barton's Yard and was at the back where the Crescent Inn and post office are now. They were altered to several small shops to face Warwick Road. Most of the alterations were carried out by Barton the coachbuilder's own workmen.

Jay Gee, November 1959

Atkinson & Davidson

Although technically not a garage, we think the firm established in 1869 by Alderman James Atkinson and now in the third generation, has for the last ninety years been actively engaged in the building and repairing of road vehicle bodies from purely horse-drawn conveyances of every kind, to the first horseless carriages, charabancs, buses, etc. to the present day cars and trucks. Having participated in the transition from horse to diesel, we feel we are probably the oldest firm in the motor industry in Cumberland.

J.K. Atkinson, Cathedral Motor Body Works, March 1959

The Tax Man

A few recollections of taxes in Carlisle sixty-five years ago, may be of interest. There was no surtax, no PAYE, no telephones, no typewriters, no typists or other female staff and no carbon copies.

E.C. Poole, retired Surveyor of Taxes, November 1970

Postmen

Postie huts were common to the rural men of the early 1890s, the time of gigs and cycles…the men had to be Spartan in nature, being subject to the elements of wind, rain and blizzards. Accommodation size could be that of a sentry box, if bigger, more of a coal-shed variety, with a brazier for coke and an egg pan. Some were very old with a few holes plugged with old bags.

You could be lucky or unlucky when consigned to a village post office, for many had a small shop attached, so you had irregular meals and you bought your own food.

Fireplaces I never saw; farmers were your best friends, for in return for small services such as haymaking or hedge-cutting [while waiting for collection times] you got a real good meal.

First aid was an asset for there were instances in which I was concerned; once a woman of seventy-six lay

with a broken leg for hours until my arrival. In another an old woman of eighty-two, feeling ill, tried to make for the front door but fell unconscious. Arriving with mail I heard her moaning and securing a farmer's assistance, we broke a pane at her back to get in and found her lying behind the locked front door. Rural postmen had to contend with everything…town postmen 'never had it so good'.

Harold Slight, 1962

Whitfield & Howe

My grandfather, John Whitfield, was the founder of Whitfield & Howe. He came from the North East to Carlisle and commenced business in Mary Street (now, I believe, demolished) somewhere about 1850. Later he went into partnership with his friend, Mr Howe, a coachbuilder whose premises were on the site now occupied by Menzies in Lowther Street. The works in Lorne Street were built and the firm of Whitfield & Howe came into being. My grandfather was responsible for the chain, hames and caulker works in Lorne Street. When my grandfather died he left his son John – my father – at the age of twenty to carry on the business, which he did for some years, eventually selling it to Joseph Fidler. After a few years in retirement, he was invited back as works manager and director, but finally retired on the death of Mr Fidler. James Harrison carried on the business for a while until he was forced to retire through illness and the Lorne Street works were finally closed down [in 1959]. The chains were

Rural postmen, like this one photographed by M. Davis of Carlisle, were very hardy and had a wealth of local knowledge. They were difficult to replace and worked on long after others had retired.

hand made and I remember very well watching Pringle, who was one of the last to make chains by hand, fascinated by the speed at which the chains took shape in his hands. The chains were used in pits and in connection with horse-drawn vehicles, until the horse was superseded by the motor.

Hames, the steel casing round the collar used by dray horses were also a profitable side of the business, but again when the motor took the place of the horse that side of the business declined. Caulkers, perhaps better known as clog irons, were made to a special pattern for this district and were in demand until the war by makers of clogs, but now, I think, there is only one clog maker in the city. My father died in 1960 at the age of ninety-five years.

Hilda Brown, May 1971

For delivering heavy parcels, it was easier for the postmen if he did his rounds on a bicycle.

Stonebreakers

If you happened to be on the back roads in these parts [around Rockliffe] you would have come across John Allen, sitting beside a long heap of stones breaking them into small pieces for road making. He was paid by the yard (so much for each yard broken). He is the last of these stone breakers that I can remember and would be about the year 1920.

Jas Maxwell, 1957

Unemployment

After ten weeks out of work I have finally got a job at Spadeadam as an electrician's mate. My first week in employment we went on strike, now I have 11 ¾ hours to lift on Wednesday and there's talk of a strike coming off again. I hope to God this does not happen as I want to get back on my feet. I only wish I could get a good job with a decent wage and no Union worry. I leave the house between 6 and 7 a.m. and get home about 7 p.m...I am so pleased to be in work again.

Norman Garnett, October 1958

Knowefield Nurseries

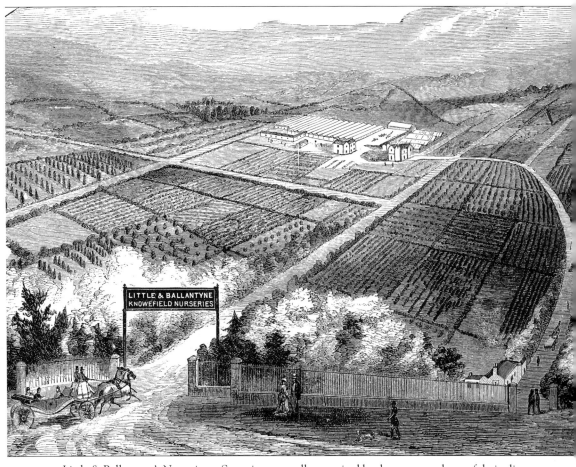

Little & Ballantyne's Nurseries at Stanwix were well patronized by the gentry and one of their clients was Queen Victoria. During the season as many as 200 workers could be seen there.

In those days of poverty and privation [1890s] quite a number of local female workers were employed there, hard as teak but willing, for they had to survive. Quite a few were local characters rejoicing in the known pseudonyms as 'Cinderella', 'Esther Jane', 'Fag Ash Lil' and the 'Stanwix Beauty'. Quick in repartee they could hold their own in a word battle with any of the wise-crackers.

Harold Slight, 1962

County Gaol

The group taken in 1912 of the officers of the old Carlisle Gaol is of great interest to me as my father, Dr Helm, is on the left of the Governor. The dog in front of Dr Helm belonged to him and was called Rock.

Commander L.R.D. Helm, March 1962

Prison Staff

CHAPTER 8

Order and government

Special constables recruited to deal with the general strike in 1926, outside the police station on West Walls.

Staff of HM Prison Carlisle grouped outside the Governor's house inside the prison in 1912. Prior to 1 April 1878, this had been the County Gaol for Cumberland.

The picture was sent in December 1951 by Mrs Holley of Ambury Hill, Huntingdon. She was the daughter of Warder D. Munday, who is on the extreme right of the back row of the group, which was taken in 1912. The Governor at that time was J.H. Briggenshaw, but I am not sure if he is the gentleman in mufti in the centre of the front row, or if he is further along the row in braided uniform and beard. I think the vicar of St Cuthbert's was the Anglican gaol chaplin and the vicar at that time was the Revd A.J.W. Crosse. I imagine he might be in the black straw boater. The other chaplins are presumably Free Church (top hat?) and Roman Catholic.

Mary Burgess, April 1962

Silent Gaol

My grandfather, John Brown, was a lay preacher in his spare time and frequently took a service in the prison. On several occasions he took me with him and I spent the time in the warden's house just inside the gates while he went across to the main prison block for the service.

The thing which I always remember was the almost complete silence which enveloped one as soon as the tiny wicket gate closed behind one.

No sound of traffic, either trams or horse-drawn, no sound even from the public house which stood just outside the walls. The silence was equalled by the desolate appearance of the prison yard, apart from the occasional warder or prisoner crossing my line of vision, the place seemed deserted.

My grandfather's feelings were usually sad on the way home. I remember him telling me how disgusted he was when as a boy he witnessed crowds jostling for a vantage point near the West Walls when a public execution was taking place.

Herbert Brown, April 1970

Prisoners' Soup

I was inside the gaol when I was a boy. My father was employed by Walter Wood, coal merchant (who had the contract to deliver coal to the gaol for heating) and he took me with him one day. I only remember sitting in a room, I presume one of the warder's rooms just inside the gates, until the coal was unloaded, meanwhile tasting the thin soup prepared for the prisoners.

J.F. Stalker, April 1970

Last Warder

About the gaol itself, there is a man called Jimmy Oliver in Miss Welsh's Home at Harraby who is the last surviving warder. He is ninety-two.

S. Turner, April 1970

The Courts

Near to a public house which was known locally as the 'Gaol Tap', I recall that Jimmy Dyer used to play his fiddle. Also that when the Assize Court was sitting, the street used to be spread with either cork chips or sawdust to ensure the noise of passing traffic did not disturb the court.

On market days there were stalls there and one in particular stands out in my memory for the stallholder sold a yellow toffee, known as 'Gaol Toffee'.

John W. Brough, April 1970

Silence in Court

Court Square with its cobbles recalls memories of the Assizes, then a thick covering of bark was put down to deaden the sound of wheels of carriages and horses hooves. On 1 October [each year] chains were put round the Square to claim it for the Caledonian Railway.

Mr E. Curr, August 1970

Carlisle Parliament

Dr Hastings Rashdall was dean of the cathedral. He was a great scholar and a great gentleman and was actively interested in working class education and welfare. I first met him when he was speaker of the Carlisle Parliament, which used to meet at the YMCA headquarters in Fisher Street. It was here that I went as a visitor one evening and had taken my seat in the visitor's gallery, when I was approached by two Members whom I

121

did not know and cajoled into allowing myself to be introduced as the Member for Cardigonshire, an election having just been fought in that constituency. I was escorted through a crowded and cheering House and presented to Mr Speaker.

This to a youngster of eighteen was somewhat of an ordeal. I remember that the chief 'Government' speaker that night was the Hon R.D. Denman, whilst the leader of the opposition was the now Lord Mathers.

Tom Lightfoot, March 1957

Stanwix Reformatory

My father, George Crowther, was the Governor of the reformatory at Stanwix, there from about 1869 to 1883. When he left he started a private school for boys known as Hanover House, Warwick Road. When we lived at Stanwix there was a master called Holiday who taught shoemaking; Robinson taught tailoring and Whitaker took boys for gardening. I remember one boy became a gardener at Brayton [Hall]. One boy went to sea and became a captain of a big ship.

Emilie Crowther, April 1956

Poachers

The Carlisle Parliament was a debating society organized as a Westminster with different parties, MPs and a Speaker.

The Cumberland and Westmorland Reformatory for Boys at Stanwix now forms part of Cumbria College of Art and Design.

One of these salmon poachers I knew well. He lived in Dudson's Court, Rickergate. He had many visits from the police and 'water watchers', but they could never find a trace of salmon in his house, simply because the salmon were in the house of an eighty-year-old lady that got her share of the spoil when the salmon was sold. Yes there were receivers in those days that made salmon poaching very profitable.

Richard Carruthers, March 1959

First Woman Magistrate

The first lady magistrate in 1920, was my mother Mrs Annie Dundas M. Fyfe. She then resided in Mulcaster Crescent, Stanwix and belonged to that band of keen local Suffragists who took part in the Pilgrimage to London [in 1913]. She was the first woman to be elected to the board of management of the Carlisle Co-operative Society; a member of the Food Control and Liquor Control Committees; was vice-president of the Workers Educational Association when it first started in Carlisle; a governor of the Cumberland Infirmary and served on many other local committees. She took a keen interest in local politics. When she died in 1948, the year of the start of the Welfare State, Herbert Atkinson, a former Mayor of Carlisle, wrote to me that the country had now got all that she had worked for. I often wonder what she would have thought of the result.

Anne D.M. Fyfe, September 1968

Black Marias

A black van was one of the Black Marias; a faithful driver with his favourite horse, wooden cross-seats with the windows protected by iron bars and a let down step at the rear.

Harold Slight, 1962

Mock Mayors

Johnny Ribchester was Mayor of Upperby in the early 1900s. He was odd-job man in the village and lived in a thatched clay cottage in what is now St Ninians Road. The ceremony was performed at the Black Bull – a pub on the corner of St Ninians Road and Brisco Road, every New Year's Day. A pony was borrowed for the mayor to make a tour of the village and make speeches. He delivered his speech at the River Petteril, the cross roads, Lamb Street and Roseland Terrace and people came from quite a distance to hear him. He told what he'd do as mayor – build houses, a railway station etc! Although he had no money! After the speeches it was back to the pub.

William Bell, February 1974

Local Lad Made Good

Lord Henderson, first Baron Ardwick, was an outstanding success story; for to have risen from being a back street boy, with only an elementary education, to the Ermine, by way of becoming Mayor of Carlisle, MP and junior Lord of the Treasury was no mean feat. Joe

Henderson as he was popularly known, was intensely proud of his native Cumberland and took his full share in any movement for its wellbeing.

Tom Lightfoot, December 1956

The Workhouse

I could only be a very young child [in the First World War]…but you see my uncle, W.S. Jardine was engineer at Fusehill [workhouse] for a record period covering both the Great War and the last one and from my earliest childhood we visited him and my aunt in their pleasant gabled house across the daisied lawn beside the chapel, at least twice a week and became friendly with scores of staff and patients [when it was a military hospital]. The hospital matron we remember best, Miss Kelsey who left Fusehill to serve with distinction in France, but returned after the war to resume her matronship of the hospital, now the City Maternity Hospital. At the same time the Big House [the main block] became once more the Union [workhouse] under Mr and Mrs Elsdon and we children formed unique but happy relationships with many of the inmates, from the gingham-gowned toddlers playing through the railings of their garden, to certain dear or droll old men who did errands for auntie.

Anne Johnson, June 1969

Elections

When Claude Lowther was fighting a General Election…someone

The infirmary wing of the Fusehill Workhouse was used as a military hospital in the First World War and later became the City Maternity Hospital.

in the audience called out, 'what about Sir Wilfred Lawson's liquor bill?' His prompt reply was, 'I don't know about Sir Wilfred's, but I know mine's a sight too much sometimes'.

Mrs A. Bushby, November 1965

A Different World

I was born in 1876. How very different the world was then! In the General Election of 1900…I remember my parents setting off for the Brampton meeting in a trap decorated with yellow ribbons [the Conservative colours for Claude Lowther]. I could not go as tickets were strictly limited, but I was asked to go to the County Hall and watch votes being counted after polling day. That was all very interesting. I

can picture it very clearly even now. Mr C. Lowther and Mr R. Graham of Beanlands Park, called to see my father at Irthington, just a few days before polling day. At the time I chanced to be at home on holiday and photographed them. Then I was very much an amateur and had to develop the photograph myself, still it has stood the test of time.

Miss Ruth Law, December 1957

Opposition

I was present at the meeting in St Martins Hall. Brampton, on 8 October 1900. The meeting was addressed by Claude Lowther, the candidate and Sir Winston (then Mr) Churchill. The usual 'fit and proper' resolution was submitted and carried with acclamation. Against, one hand was raised, which caused Mr Lowther to remark 'Ah, I see my friend Lady Carlisle' [she being a renowned Liberal]. At that time I was employed in the building of the new Methodist chapel in Moatside, Brampton.

Wm Jas Herbertson, December 1957

Canvassing

Claude Lowther's election campaign was one of the most hilarious that could be envisaged. Bouts were fought by opposing parties and canvassing was carried out with the utmost intenseness. Mrs Margaret Thompson of Little Corby Farm, canvassed with whip in hand and woe betide any villager who dare say he was not a supporter of *her* man, as she put it. A slash of the whip around the legs was the price for daring.

A commotion took place in the Commons after his maiden speech. [He was a crack shot and a good huntsman]. An opposite member rose to his feet and asked 'Was there any rabbits or ducks about?' The House rocked with laughter.

John Forster, November 1957

Claude Lowther

I will come back to Know-Know- Flo

Claude Lowther in the uniform of the Imperial Yeomanry, in which he served in the Boer War. He was elected the Conservative MP for the Eskdale Division of Cumberland in 1900, a seat he held until 1906. He died unmarried in 1929.

Temperance

Sir Wilfred Lawson, I never missed the opportunity to hear him speak on the great subjects of Peace and Temperance. I recall a peace meeting in the Town Hall, a huge crowd. He had much opposition, but he held his own against all comers. He was one of the few MPs who voted against the war in South Africa.

In 1902 or 1903 I heard him speak before a large audience in Penrith. A man 'brimful of the spirit' had gained admission to the meeting in order to create a row. There were cries of 'Put him out'. 'No, no', replied Sir Wilfred, 'let him stay – he will help me – he is full of my subject'.

When he first contested Carlisle he was a very young man. He was told to go home to his mother. 'I cannot help my age – but I will grow older.'

Sir Wilfred Lawson in old age. He was a Liberal MP for Carlisle and was a great advocate of Temperance. Later he was MP for Cockermouth. He died in 1906.

Richard Graham, June 1963

No Loudspeakers

I heard W.E. Gladstone speak from a balcony in front of the County Hotel in Court Square [in 1890]. There were no loudspeakers then but one heard him as far as the top of the square.

R. Baxter, December 1957

In Reflection

This is a very humble account of things I remember and it has been a pleasure writing it. Times have changed; we have wireless, television and rock and roll, but whether we are any happier it would be hard to say.

Jas Maxwell, 1957

Expatriot Clubs

I belonged to the Cumberland & Westmorland Association in Birmingham 'til it was disbanded during the last war. It was a good link with home and I met lots of Carlisle people and thoroughly enjoyed the Cumberland accent and style of those people of the North.

Mary Lenton, March 1957

The Unionist Party office in Carlisle. Posters show the Unionist stance on various issues during a General Election campaign in the Edwardian era.

Miss E. Armstrong, November 1970.

Changing City

I thought…that maybe at some future time it may be of interest if you are recalling the past again. I am interested in Carlisle and I am only too sorry that it appears to be gradually losing its character to modernity and becoming just another repetition of many other towns with their multiple supermarkets and chain stores. I suppose these changes are to a great extent inevitable and provided they do not, or are not allowed to change the Carlisle that was, all we can do is accept them, however unwillingly.